Vegan
Chocoholic

Philip Hochuli

Vegan
Chocoholic

Cakes, Biscuits,
Desserts and Quick Sweet Snacks

Grub Street • London

Published in 2016 by Grub Street
4 Rainham Close
London
SW11 6SS

Email: food@grubstreet.co.uk
Web: www.grubstreet.co.uk
Twitter: @grub_street
Facebook: Grub Street Publishing

Photos: Alexandra Schubert, www.myshoots.de
Image editing: Vogt-Schild Druck, Derendingen

A CIP record for this title is available from the British Library.

ISBN 978-1-910690-32-1

Printed and bound by Finidr, Czech Republic

Contents

Foreword

'A day without chocolate – unthinkable!'

Dear chocoholics

Few foods or beverages are as alluring and fascinating as chocolate, and not just for every generation, but also in almost every nation.

This book will take you on a culinary adventure through the world of chocolate. Had the word 'vegan' not appeared in its title, you would hardly suspect that this book contained purely vegan recipes, but this was always my intention. As regards taste, vegan cuisine is in no way inferior to the 'classics'. Rather, my experience even shows that the opposite is true: vegan cuisine represents an enormous culinary enrichment. The fact is that there is no need for sacrifice, particularly as far as sweet creations are concerned, and that chocolate's place in vegan cuisine is at least as important as it is in conventional cuisine, as this book demonstrates in some sixty recipes.

Personally, the most important thing is to have fun with cooking and baking, which I think are some of the nicest things you can do, an area in which I've been involved in professionally for several years. The subject of this book is a food preparation that has an extremely important place in my life.

A day without chocolate for me would be incomplete. I've never been as enthusiastic about any other food as I have about chocolate.

The recipes in this book range from classic cakes and biscuits to exquisite dessert creations and quick and delicious treats such as truffles, pralines and home-made chocolate yoghurt. Refined chocolate can also be used in spicy dishes, as shown in a small selection of savoury main courses. You won't find any fancy ingredients or long ingredient lists. You should be able to find between 95-98 per cent of the ingredients in supermarkets. Most of the recipes have a very simple design and are really simple to make. I consider these two points to be the most important things to ensure the recipes are suitable for daily use and that the joy of cooking isn't spoilt by endless instructions. My personal tip: leaf through the pages, and when the urge takes you, just cook – in that order. Information on the level of difficulty and preparation time is provided to help you decide.

The book is completed with an introductory section offering important information on chocolate and practical tips for cooking. You should always pay attention to this advice before starting on the recipe. I won't go into why going vegan can or should make sense. If you're a vegan, you already know; and if you want to know about it, there's plenty of information available on the Internet and in books. What I find fascinating about vegan cuisine is the incredible variation and diversity of flavours, and the fact that vegan dishes are simply a lot of fun to make. That's what I want to convey in this book.

And finally: This book isn't a guide to healthy living and is definitely not a book for people looking to get fit. Its purpose is to bring you fun and pleasure. And one more thing: Don't forget to wipe off the chocolate from around your mouth before you leave home…

Introduction

About the recipes

The recipes in this book are marked according to their difficulty with stars, with 1 star being the lowest level and 3 stars representing the highest level of difficulty. The stars and the preparation time are a good indication of the effort required for each recipe. The fact that very few recipes have 3 stars demonstrates the basic idea behind the book and the suitability of the recipes for everyday use.

Unless otherwise stated, the following information applies to baking: Bake on the middle shelf with top and bottom heat, in conventional (static) oven mode.

The recipes that contain no gluten, soya or sugar are marked with the following symbols:

 = gluten free

 = soya free (alternative ingredients: almond milk instead of soya milk)

 = sugar free (refined sugar)

Some important ingredients

Bourbon vanilla powder (ground vanilla pods)
This product is a great alternative to vanilla pods and is particularly easy to use, since you don't have to split a pod and scrape out the seeds every time. Vanilla powder is found in small jars and available in super-markets and organic food shops. Tightly closed, it keeps almost indefinitely. In these recipes, vanilla powder can always be substituted by vanilla pods and vice versa. Convert with this rule: The seeds from a vanilla pod are equivalent to ⅓ of a teaspoon of vanilla powder.

Cocoa powder
In a book focussing on nothing but chocolate, a good cocoa powder is essential. Bear this in mind when buying a particularly high-quality product. On no account should cocoa powder be confused with chocolate powder. The latter contains cocoa and other ingredients, mainly sugar. It's also important to distinguish between the lightly defatted variety (about 20 g/¾ oz fat for every 100 g/3¾ oz) and the extensively defatted variety (about 10 g/¼ oz fat for every 100 g). The lightly defatted variety has an intense flavour and more rounded mouthfeel, which is why it is used exclusively in my recipes (more on this can be found on p. 13). The labelling doesn't clearly state which variety it contains, so it's useful to check the fat content provided on the package.

Coconut oil
Coconut oil is one of the few fats or oils that is solid at room temperature. For this reason, and because it withstands high temperatures, it is very popular for use in cooking. The choice is between the cold-pressed or virgin form of the oil, which has a very strong coconut flavour, and refined oil, which has a relatively neutral taste. The latter can be found in most supermarkets. Unless otherwise stated on the package, you can assume it isn't cold pressed. Virgin coconut oils are available at gourmet and organic food shops. I very rarely use virgin coconut oil because its intense coconut flavour is usually undesirable in dishes, and coconut oil is typically used for its other qualities. Owing to this difference in flavour, virgin coconut oil should on no account be used as a substitute for

refined coconut oil, otherwise the dish will most likely be unsuccessful. Unlike cold-pressed coconut oil, coconut oil with the additional labelling of 'mild' can be used.

Flour

Choosing the right flour plays an important and decisive role in my recipes. Two particular points need to be taken into consideration:

The type of grain and the extraction rate.

The importance of the type of grain: The recipes basically use wheat flour or the alternative of spelt flour, as these have the best properties for baking and binding of all different types of flour. The use of other flours with these recipes might result in unpleasant surprises. In the case of gluten intolerance, use special flours that are as close as possible to the properties of wheat or spelt flours.

The importance of extraction rate: A distinction is usually made between the extraction rate, or the quantity of the whole grain used, between flours with low extraction rate (light flour) and flours with a high extraction rate (dark flour). Light (white) wheat and spelt flours have excellent baking and binding properties, particularly the latter, so they can easily be used to replace eggs in certain recipes, which is important for vegan cuisine. These are also the flours of choice for the recipes in this book. I get the best results in baking using white wheat flour. This is the equivalent of plain flour, pastry flour or cake flour.

Neutral vegetable oil

These include liquid plant oils with little or no taste and therefore will not influence the flavour of dishes.

There are many different commercially available oils that meet this requirement. The following oils have been tried and tested in my kitchen: neutral, refined sunflower oil for low and medium temperatures; high oleic sunflower oil and refined peanut (groundnut) oil for high temperatures.

Plant-based milk

Plant-based alternatives to cow's milk range from the well-known but – as far as taste is concerned – questionable soya milk and others made from spelt, rice and oats to almond and cashew milk. The choice depends on different factors. When it comes to baking and cooking, soya, almond and cashew milks are suitable. The characteristics of rice, spelt and oat milks mean that they aren't ideal for cooking or baking, and I don't recommend them. Soya milk is the easiest to work with, as its protein and fat content is the closest to cow's milk. Its questionable flavour almost completely evaporates during cooking or baking, making it extremely versatile.

Certain recipes require the use of soya milk because their success depends on its protein content, and the other alternatives contain no protein. For example, this applies to the lemon and 'cream cheese' slice and the saffron cream pie.

Vegan margarine

In a book with a large proportion of baked dishes, margarine plays an important part. Margarines can be found in any supermarket. However, many of them unexpectedly contain dairy ingredients, so it's a good idea to check the list of ingredients. Given that cheap margarines contain trans (hydrogenated) fats, and also because of the environmentally questionable use of palm oil, an ingredient in practically all margarines, the question is whether there is an alternative to margarine. In my culinary experience, there's no alternative to margarine; coconut oil isn't a suitable alternative, and so far there are practically no palm oil-free margarines on the market. There is now a butter-flavoured rapeseed oil that can replace margarine in some recipes, but by no means in all of them. The environmentally questionable use of palm oil can be overcome by purchasing organic margarine certified by reliable organic labels, made with environmentally friendly palm oil. As for avoiding unhealthy trans fats, simply don't go for the cheap margarines, because usually only the cheapest margarines contain these discredited fatty acids. So it's worth having a good look on the back of the package.

Vegan dark chocolate

Besides cocoa, good vegan dark chocolate is the essential ingredient in a book on chocolate. It is therefore fundamental to ensure the use of a high-quality product. I always recommend Swiss chocolate, not because I'm being patriotic, but because qualitative experience has shown that it's in fact very difficult to beat. Cheap cooking chocolate should not be used; as with other ingredients, care must be taken with quality. There's also vegan milk and white chocolate. Since it's always important that my recipes are designed for everyday use, neither is used in my recipes. These products are sometimes available in organic food shops, but are often only found in gourmet shops and online.

Chocolate: Essentials, Production and Products

From bean to chocolate

'In the beginning was the bean' is more or less how it goes. This is how the story of chocolate starts. However, there are many steps in the manufacturing process that takes the harvested cocoa beans to the three main end products of cocoa butter, cocoa powder and chocolate confectionery. The following is a brief outline of the main steps and a description of the individual intermediate and end products, which are also of interest for the recipes.

The cocoa bean – where it all begins

Cocoa beans are the starting point for each of the following products. The main producers of cocoa beans are Ivory Coast, Ghana and Indonesia. Cocoa beans themselves can actually be eaten (the broken up beans are known as cocoa nibs), although this use is not widespread and, for many, it takes a lot of getting used to. The beans are a valuable and appreciated resource that further processing will turn into a series of products. The cocoa beans are prepared for further processing by cleaning and roasting. Basically, roasting brings out the aroma of chocolate, making this an essential step. The beans are then shelled and ready for the next step in the process.

Cocoa mass

The roasted and shelled beans are milled and turned into a liquid, known as cocoa mass or cocoa liquor. This is only an intermediate product and forms the base of the subsequent production of cocoa butter, cocoa powder and, finally, chocolate confectionery, which will involve more processing with additional cocoa butter and, depending on the type of chocolate, with a wide variety of other ingredients.

Cocoa butter

Cocoa butter is the oil extracted from cocoa mass. Cocoa butter is solid at room temperature and ideally should not contain any water, which is why it's also suitable for use where it needs to be melted with chocolate (unlike butter or margarine; for more see 'the correct way to heat and melt chocolate' on p. 14). Cocoa butter is a yellowish-white colour, which is a surprise for many who see it for the first time. It is the same colour as white chocolate, which is no coincidence, since the two products are directly related. Only cocoa butter goes into white chocolate. No cocoa powder is used. This is why white chocolate has the characteristic colour of cocoa butter and not the dark colour of cocoa powder. The following principle basically applies: the lighter the chocolate, the higher the proportion of cocoa butter.

Cocoa powder

Aside from chocolate confectionery, cocoa powder is probably the most widely used and popular product made from cocoa beans. It's extremely versatile, easy to use and immediately adds a wonderful chocolatey aroma. After the cocoa butter is extracted from cocoa mass, cocoa powder is left as a dry product. Unlike cocoa butter, cocoa powder has a dark, chocolatey colour. Depending on how thoroughly the cocoa mass is defatted, i.e. depending on how much cocoa butter is extracted from it, the result is lightly defatted or extensively defatted cocoa powder. The difference between both varieties is very significant. Lightly defatted cocoa powder is characterised by an intense and rounded flavour, while the extensively defatted variety is more soluble in water owing to its lower residual oil content, and is therefore more widely used in beverages. My recipes only make use of lightly defatted cocoa powder.

Chocolate as an end product

It is a long process to make the internationally prized and popular end product that is high-quality chocolate. After the desired amount of cocoa butter and any other ingredients are added to the cocoa mass, the process involves quite a few more steps. The first step is about achieving a fine texture. Absolutely no rough lumps should be felt on the tongue that will spoil the enjoyment of the chocolate. To achieve this, the chocolate is passed through several rollers and, depending on preference, is rolled down to thinness of a few micrometres. Only this refining process will ensure that the chocolate will feel soft as it melts in the mouth, and not have a rough feel. The final two steps are conching and tempering. Broadly speaking, the first of these steps involves the chocolate being heated to a high temperature and mixed for many hours. The aim of this is to allow any moisture to escape and to achieve a smooth flavour. The last step, tempering, is ultimately responsible for the chocolate having the right crystalline structure. Last but not least, it gives chocolate its characteristic gloss and the popping sound we expect from a good chocolate when broken. Crystals can form in as many as six different ways, but only one is desirable. After conching, tempering involves gentle, precise and controlled cooling of the chocolate and temporarily maintaining the liquid chocolate at a certain temperature. The conched and tempered chocolate is then poured into the desired mould and slowly allowed to cool, before being packaged. Depending on the cocoa mass content, a distinction is made between white, milk and dark chocolate.

The correct way to heat and melt chocolate

How to melt chocolate the right way and why in certain circumstances there can be undesirable results from the melting process are questions that are often asked. Here is a quick lesson on the basics of melting chocolate correctly.

There are two ways of melting chocolate: the conventional way over a bain-marie, and in a microwave.

When melting chocolate over a bain-marie, the bowl should not come into contact with the water; the chocolate is melted slowly by the rising steam. The best thing is to use a chrome-plated steel bowl that is a bit larger than the diameter of the saucepan. Chrome-plated steel distributes the heat the best and ensures even melting. The chocolate should be stirred gently, so that not too many air bubbles will form in the chocolate. For this reason, a rubber scraper or spatula is better for stirring than a whisk.

Melting chocolate in the microwave is very popular and is often the easier option. Caution: Use a low setting and check from time to time that the bottom of the bowl isn't too hot. Otherwise, there is a risk of burning the chocolate. Here's another tip: The more finely you chop the chocolate before melting, the more evenly it will melt, both in the microwave and over a bain-marie.

Regardless of the option you choose, there are two basic principles that you need to bear in mind.

1. Chocolate is extremely sensitive to heat and should be melted slowly on a low heat or at a low setting. Ideally, dark chocolate should never be heated to over 40°C/104°F. Milk chocolate requires a lower temperature. The molecular structure of chocolate can be modified at high temperatures, causing it to thicken, for instance. This may not be so important for most of the recipes as the melted chocolate will be incorporated into a mixture anyway. However, it is important in two cases: when the recipe calls for very runny melted chocolate (for example, the chocolate sushi), or when the melted chocolate is going to be cooled again to give it the same properties as chocolate confectionery, for instance, if you ever want to make your own chocolates.

2. Chocolate and water don't get on well. The addition of water or ingredients with a high water content (such as milk or soya milk) causes the chocolate to thicken, or even worse, the cocoa butter to separate from the rest of the chocolate, giving it a gritty consistency.

If this happens, the chocolate is beyond saving, so you'll have to start over again. This is the reason for using cocoa powder when making cakes. The batter is usually made with ingredients that contain a lot of water. And this is also why the bowl should completely cover the saucepan when melting chocolate over a bain-marie. Otherwise, there's a risk that steam will enter the bowl of chocolate and ruin the result.

If the chocolate for a recipe has to be very runny or needs to retain its original qualities, it's essential to ensure that no water, steam or any ingredients that contain water come into contact with the chocolate.

3. This principle also applies, at least in theory, for melting chocolate together with margarine. As margarine contains some water (as does butter), there's also a risk that the chocolate will thicken. Chocolate should only be melted with margarine if any possible thickening doesn't pose a problem for the recipe, such as when making a cake. Chocolate that has thickened, and even chocolate that has passed its use-by date are suitable for this use. It is common to combine chocolate with margarine to 'lighten' the chocolate or to give it the aroma of butter, and you will find a number of recipes in this book where chocolate and margarine are melted together. Of course, this is only possible when thickening isn't a problem for the finished product.

4. A tip for making a simple version of 'lightened' dark chocolate without the risk of thickening and without the use of margarine: cocoa butter makes an excellent alternative. Cocoa butter is available in organic food shops, gourmet food shops and online.

Spreads
and Jams

Vegan Nutella

This vegan nut spread can keep in the refrigerator for several weeks and will gain in intensity.

Makes 1 jar
Difficulty *
Preparation time: 5 minutes
        plus cooling time

75 g /3 oz vegan dark chocolate (45–55 % cocoa solids)
60 g/5 tbsp vegan margarine
75 g/6 tbsp hazelnut butter (see tip)
30 ml/2 tbsp agave syrup or 40 g/⅓ cup sifted icing sugar
5 g/1 tsp white almond butter (optional)

Slowly melt the chocolate with the margarine over a bain-marie. Add the hazelnut butter and agave syrup or icing sugar, keeping the bowl over the bain-marie.

Use a whisk to stir the mixture until there are no lumps. Optionally, add white almond butter and stir again. Remove from the heat, pour into the jar and leave to cool. (Picture on p. 17)

Tips

As an alternative to hazelnut butter, lightly toast 65 g/ 9 tbsp of ground hazelnuts in a non-stick frying pan for 2–3 minutes and add to the melted chocolate. You can also add finely chopped nuts to the finished spread to make a 'crunchy' version.

This spread also makes a wonderful filling for the chocolate yeast rolls (see p. 82).

Pages 16/17 clockwise from the left:
Dark Chocolate and Orange Cream,
Dark Chocolate Spread, Chocolate
Coconut Spread, Vegan Nutella

Dark Chocolate Spread 🌾 🐝

You can make this recipe for a delicious vegan dark chocolate spread in a flash. It also has a very long shelf life when stored outside the refrigerator.

Makes 1 jar
Difficulty ✳
Preparation time: 5 minutes plus
    cooling time

90 g/7 tbsp refined coconut oil
90 g/¾ cup sifted icing sugar
40 g/⅓ cup lightly defatted cocoa
    powder (see tip)
1 pinch salt
1 pinch Bourbon vanilla powder
    (optional)

Slowly heat the coconut oil in a frying pan until completely melted. Add the other ingredients and stir with a whisk to a smooth cream. Remove from the heat, pour into the jar and leave to cool. The spread is quite creamy at room temperature and will firm up in the refrigerator. (Picture on p. 16)

Tip

I prefer to use 50 g/½ cup of cocoa powder because I like a strong taste of chocolate. But if you prefer a milder flavour, use 40 g/⅓ cup.

Chocolate Coconut Spread 🌾 🐝

Makes 1 small jar
Difficulty ✳
Preparation time: 5 minutes plus cooling
    time

75 g/⅔ cup sifted icing sugar
4 tbsp coconut milk, or another plant-
    based milk
50 g/¼ cup cold-pressed coconut oil (see
    tip)
4 tsp desiccated coconut
1 pinch salt
2 tbsp lightly defatted cocoa powder

Dissolve the icing sugar completely in the coconut milk. Heat the coconut oil until it is completely melted. Add the other ingredients and stir everything well with a whisk. Allow to cool, and then fill a jar.

The spread is quite creamy at room temperature and will firm up in the refrigerator. Although it needs to be stored in the refrigerator, it should be taken out some time before use. The spread will keep in the refrigerator for about 2 weeks. (Picture on p. 17)

Tip

The use of unrefined coconut oil will give this spread a strong coconut flavour. If you can't find virgin coconut oil, you can use refined coconut oil, but the coconut flavour won't be so intense.

In that case, you'll have to use coconut milk instead of another plant-based milk.

Dark Chocolate and Orange Cream 🌾 🐝

This cream is really quick to make and is the perfect topping for bread or pancakes.

Makes 1 small jar
Difficulty ✳
Preparation time: 5 minutes plus at
    least 2 hours cooling time

50 g/¼ cup vegan margarine or refined
    coconut oil
75 g/⅔ cup sifted icing sugar
50 ml/¼ cup freshly squeezed orange
    juice
25 g/¼ cup lightly defatted cocoa
    powder
1 pinch salt
⅛ tsp Bourbon vanilla powder

Melt the margarine in a saucepan or in the microwave. Dissolve the icing sugar completely in the orange juice. Add all the ingredients to the melted margarine and stir with a whisk.

Pour into a jar and leave to cool for at least 2 hours. Stir well before use. This cream can keep in the refrigerator for about 1 week.
(Picture on p. 16)

Quick Strawberry Jam with Dark Chocolate 🌾 🐝

Makes 1 jar
Difficulty ✳
Preparation time: 10 minutes plus cooling
    time

250 g/2 cups ripe strawberries
1 tbsp freshly squeezed lemon juice
200 g/⅞ cup jam sugar
40 g/1½ oz vegan dark chocolate
    (45–55 % cocoa solids)

Wash, pat dry and hull the strawberries, and purée thoroughly with a hand-held blender. Mix with the lemon juice and jam sugar, and then combine with the chocolate in a saucepan. Bring to the boil and leave to boil for 5 minutes over a medium to high heat. Immediately pour into a clean jar and seal tightly. Leave to cool. Store in the refrigerator after opening.

Quick Strawberry Jam with Dark Chocolate

Caramel Royale Sauce
with Chocolate Shavings

Caramel lovers would love to bathe in this sauce. The sauce tastes good on pancakes, cakes, muffins, bread, or just on a spoon.

Makes 1 jar

Difficulty ✳✳

Preparation time: 10 minutes plus
at least 2 hours cooling time

200 ml/scant 1 cup coconut milk
150 g/⅝ cup sugar
1 dash lemon juice
100 g/3¾ oz vegan dark chocolate
(45–55 % cocoa solids)

Combine 100 ml/scant ½ cup of coconut milk with the sugar and lemon juice in a saucepan and bring to the boil over a high heat. Slightly reduce the heat while keeping at a vigorous boil, and stir constantly with a whisk until the colour changes from white to light brown (this should take about 5 minutes). Be very careful because this change is very sudden. When hardly any more bubbles come up, this is a sign that it is almost ready.

Then continue to cook until the caramel turns a deep golden colour. If you remove the caramel from the heat too soon, it will be too light and its flavour won't be very intense, but you don't want it to cook for too long and become too dark.

Now add the rest of the coconut milk, return the saucepan to the heat and stir the sauce constantly for 2 minutes until smooth. Pour the sauce into a jar, leave to cool, and then refrigerate for at least 2 hours.

Finely chop or grate the chocolate, fold into the sauce and return it to the refrigerator. Stir briefly before each use.

Tip

Making caramel takes a little practice, so don't despair if it isn't perfect the first time.

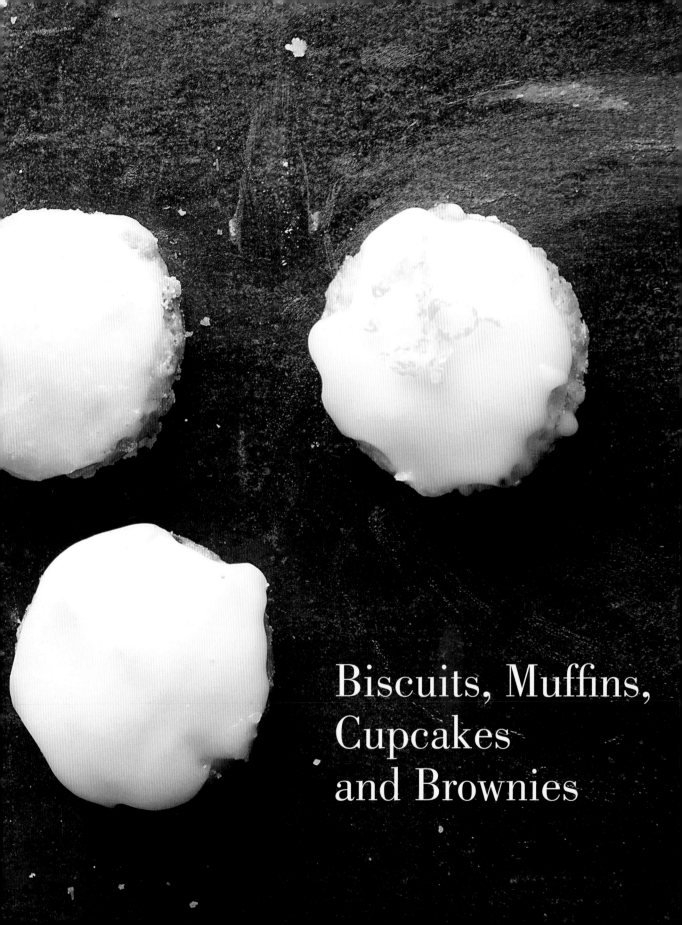

Biscuits, Muffins,
Cupcakes
and Brownies

Best-Ever American Brownies

Raspberry and Chocolate Brownies

Best-Ever American Brownies

Makes 20–30
Difficulty ✳
Preparation time: 10 minutes plus
    25-35 minutes baking time

115 g/1 cup shelled walnuts
150 g/5 oz vegan dark chocolate (45–55 % cocoa
    solids)
290 g/2½ cups light wheat or spelt flour
300 g/1¼ cups sugar
1½ tsp baking powder
90 g/¾ cup lightly defatted cocoa powder
1 tsp Bourbon vanilla powder
1 level tsp salt
2 tsp white wine vinegar
200 ml/scant 1 cup refined rapeseed oil

Preheat the oven to 180°C/350°F.

Coarsely chop the walnuts and lightly roast in a dry frying pan. They shouldn't turn too dark, but they should develop the typical roasted aroma.

Coarsely or finely chop the chocolate, according to preference, and mix together with all the dry ingredients in a bowl, including the roasted walnuts. Add 250 ml/1 cup of water, the vinegar and oil and beat together briskly until smooth.

Spread out the mixture over a baking tray lined with baking parchment to form a 30 x 33 cm/12 x 13 in rectangle, and bake for 25-35 minutes. After cooling, cut into squares of the desired size. The brownies should still be a little moist. (Picture on p. 26)

Raspberry and Chocolate Brownies

Makes 20–30
Difficulty ✳
Preparation time: 10 minutes plus
    25–30 minutes baking time

290 g/2½ cups light wheat or spelt flour
75 g/⅔ cup lightly defatted cocoa powder
2 (10 g/0.35 oz) sachets vanilla sugar
1 level tsp salt
150 g/⅝ cup sugar
2 tsp baking powder
125 g/4½ oz vegan dark chocolate (45–55 % cocoa
    solids), grated or finely chopped
250 g/scant 1 cup seedless raspberry jam (see tip)
200 ml/scant 1 cup neutral vegetable oil
1 tsp white wine vinegar
215 g/1¾ cups raspberries, fresh or frozen

Preheat the oven to 180°C/350°F.

Mix all the dry ingredients in a bowl. Add the jam, oil, vinegar and 200 ml/scant 1 cup of water, and mix well. Carefully fold the raspberries into the batter.

Spread out the mixture over a baking tray lined with baking parchment to form a 30 x 33 cm/12 x 13 in rectangle, and bake for 25–30 minutes. After cooling, cut into squares of the desired size. The brownies should still be a little moist. (Picture on p. 27)

Tip

If you can't find seedless raspberry jam, you can use normal raspberry jam and press it through a fine sieve.

Banana and Dark Chocolate Volcano

Makes 9-12
Difficulty ✻
Preparation time: 10 minutes plus
    22–25 minutes baking time

3 medium bananas
225 g/1 cup sugar
1 pinch salt
50 ml/¼ cup neutral vegetable oil
240 g/2 cups plus 2 tbsp light wheat or spelt flour
1½ tsp baking powder
9–12 tsp dark chocolate spread (see recipe on p. 19
    or use another dark chocolate spread)
Vegan chocolate sprinkles or grated vegan dark
    chocolate for sprinkling (optional, as needed)

Preheat the oven to 180°C/350°F.

Peel the bananas, put into a shallow dish and mash as finely as possible with a fork. Whisk together with the sugar, salt and oil.

Mix the flour and baking powder together, combine with the banana mixture and mix to make a batter. Put a small amount of batter into the bottom of 9–12 greased cavities of a muffin mould, and then add 1 scant teaspoon of dark chocolate spread. Cover each with 1½–2 teaspoons of batter. The muffins can be sprinkled with chocolate sprinkles or finely grated chocolate.

Bake for 22–25 minutes. The chocolate centres should have broken through the surface by the time the muffins have finished baking. If this is not the case, the chocolate would have been placed too far down inside the mould or there would have been too much batter placed over the top.
(Picture on p. 30)

Gingerbread Cake

This gingerbread cake is quick
to make.

Difficulty ✻
Preparation time: 15 minutes plus
    about 20 minutes baking time

For the gingerbread:
240 g/2 cups plus 2 tbsp wholemeal spelt flour or
    wholemeal wheat flour
150 g/⅝ cup whole cane sugar
2 tbsp gingerbread spice blend
1½ tsp baking powder
1 heaped tbsp lightly defatted cocoa powder
1 pinch salt
250 ml/1 cup soya milk
2 tbsp neutral vegetable oil

For the icing:
125 g/4¼ oz vegan dark chocolate (45–55 % cocoa
    solids)
50 g/¼ cup vegan margarine

Preheat the oven to 180°C/350°F.

Mix the dry ingredients in a bowl. Add the soya milk and oil, and mix well. Spread out the mixture over a baking tray lined with baking parchment to form a 20 x 30 cm/8 x 12 in rectangle, and bake for 20 minutes. Prick with a wooden skewer. It should come out clean when you pull it out. Otherwise, bake for a few more minutes.

For the icing, completely melt the chocolate with the margarine over a bain-marie. Spread evenly over the gingerbread and leave to cool.

Cut the gingerbread cake into rectangles. Store in a metal box or plastic container.
(Picture on p. 31)

Banana and Dark Chocolate Volcano

Gingerbread Cake

Lemon and Chocolate Chip Mini Muffins

Refreshing little muffins! Use fresh lemons for this recipe,
to give them their special flavour. If you want to make full-sized muffins,
double the ingredients to make the same number of them.

Makes about 20
Difficulty *
Preparation time: 15 minutes plus
  about 20 minutes baking time

For the muffins:
190 g/1⅔ cups light wheat or spelt flour
150 g/⅝ cup sugar
25 g/1 oz vegan dark chocolate chips or
25 g/1 oz vegan dark chocolate (44–55 %
  cocoa), chopped
1 tsp baking powder
1 pinch salt
1 untreated lemon
  for grated zest and 3 tbsp juice
3 tbsp neutral vegetable oil
100 ml/scant ½ cup soya milk

For the icing:
90 g/¾ cup icing sugar
2–3 tsp lemon juice

Preheat the oven to 180°C/350°F.

To make the batter, mix all the dry ingredients together with the lemon zest. Add the oil, lemon juice and soya milk, and mix well. Fill the greased cavities of a mini muffin mould with the batter and bake for 20 minutes (a little longer for full-sized muffins).

For the icing, mix the icing sugar with the lemon juice until smooth. The icing should be thick, so be very careful when measuring out the lemon juice. Spread the icing over the still warm muffins, and then leave the muffins to cool.

Chestnut Muffins
with a Chocolate and Cinnamon Glaze

Makes 8–10

Difficulty *

Preparation time: 15 minutes plus
    20–25 minutes baking time

For the muffins:

100 g/⅜ cup sugar

150 g/1¼ cups light wheat or spelt flour

1 tbsp baking powder

1 pinch salt

2 tsp white wine vinegar

200 g/⅔ cup frozen chestnut purée, thawed (see
    tip)

4 tbsp neutral vegetable oil

150ml/⅔ cup almond or soya milk

For the icing:

80 g/3¼ oz vegan dark chocolate (45–55 % cocoa
    solids)

20 g/1½ tbsp vegan margarine

1 tsp ground cinnamon

Vegan chocolate sprinkles (optional, as needed)

Preheat the oven to 180°C/350°F.

For the batter, combine the sugar, flour, baking powder and salt in a bowl, and mix well. In a separate bowl, combine the vinegar, chestnut purée, oil and almond or soya milk, and mix to a smooth cream.

Combine both mixtures and mix well to make a batter. Divide the batter evenly into 8–10 greased cavities of a muffin mould. Bake for 20–25 minutes.

For the icing, slowly melt the chocolate with the margarine over a bain-marie or in the microwave. Mix in the cinnamon, and then spread the icing over the still warm muffins. The muffins can be decorated with chocolate sprinkles.

Leave to cool.

Tip

Chestnut purée is best bought frozen. If this isn't available, you can replace it as follows: Make a purée by blending vacuum sealed, cooked sweet chestnuts with a little sugar (1 tablespoon per 115 g/1 cup) and water. You can make a larger amount than you need, and then freeze the rest so that you have some on hand.

Chocolate Muffins with a Liquid Centre

Makes 4
Difficulty *
Preparation time: 10 minutes plus
  10–13 minutes baking time

80 g/3¼ oz vegan dark chocolate (45–55 % cocoa solids)
50 g/¼ cup vegan margarine
50 g/¼ cup sugar
90 g/¾ cup light wheat or spelt flour
2 tsp baking powder
1 pinch salt
1 tsp white wine vinegar

Preheat the oven to 180°C/350°F.

Slowly melt the chocolate with the margarine over a bain-marie or in the microwave.

Mix the dry ingredients in a bowl. Add the melted chocolate mixture, 3 tablespoons of water and the vinegar, and mix slowly but thoroughly.

Divide the batter into four individual ramekins or cups (if baked in a mould with individual cavities, line with muffin cases). Bake for 10–13 minutes. The centres should still be liquid. Serve immediately. (Picture on p. 36)

Chocolate Amaretti

Makes about 16
Difficulty *
Preparation time: 15 minutes plus
  14–18 minutes baking time

100 g/generous ¾ cup ground almonds
100 g/generous ¾ cup sifted icing sugar
40 g/⅓ cup light wheat or spelt flour
1 tsp baking powder
½ tsp cornflour
1 large pinch salt
1½ tbsp neutral vegetable oil
50 ml/¼ cup almond or soya milk
2–3 dashes lemon juice
½ tsp bitter almond flavouring
35 g/1¼ oz vegan dark chocolate (45–55 % cocoa solids), finely grated
20 g/¾ oz vegan dark chocolate, melted (optional)

Preheat the oven to 200°C/400°F.

Mix the ground almonds, icing sugar, flour, baking powder, cornflour and salt in a bowl. Add the oil, soya or almond milk, lemon juice and bitter almond flavouring, and mix briskly until smooth. Finally, fold the finely grated chocolate into the batter.

On a baking tray lined with baking parchment, make about 16 small mounds, spaced out evenly over the tray and with sufficient space around them, as they will expand as they bake.

Bake the amaretti for 14–18 minutes, and then leave to cool. Optionally, fill a clean plastic bag with the melted chocolate. Cut out a small hole and pipe chocolate over the amaretti. Leave to cool again. (Picture on p. 37)

Chocolate Muffin with a Liquid Centre

Chocolate Amaretti

Chocolate and Peanut Muffins

Makes 10-14

Difficulty **

Preparation time: 25 minutes plus
    14–17 minutes baking time

For the muffins:

125 g/generous ½ cup sugar

175 g/1½ cups light wheat or spelt flour

2 tbsp lightly defatted cocoa powder

1 large pinch salt

1½ tsp baking powder

50 g/2 oz vegan dark chocolate, chopped

1 tbsp cornflour

75 ml/⅓ cup cold water

120 ml/½ cup neutral vegetable oil

1 tsp white wine vinegar

For the icing:

110 g/½ cup peanut butter

50 g/4 tbsp soft vegan margarine (leave out of
    the refrigerator to soften before use)

115 g/1 cup sifted icing sugar

⅔ tsp salt

1–2 tsp plant-based milk

Chopped peanuts and grated chocolate to
    sprinkle (optional, as needed)

Preheat the oven to 190°C/375°F.

For the muffins, mix the sugar, flour, cocoa powder, salt, baking powder and chopped chocolate together in a bowl. Dissolve the cornflour completely in cold water, and add together with the oil and vinegar to the flour mixture. Mix well to obtain a smooth batter. If the batter is too dry, add a little more water.

Line 10–14 cavities of a muffin mould with muffin cases and fill with the batter. Bake for 14–17 minutes. The muffin centres should still be moist after baking.

For the icing, mix the peanut butter and margarine until smooth. Add the icing sugar, salt and milk, and beat to a fluffy cream. If the icing is too runny, add more icing sugar; and if it's too firm, add more milk.

Use a piping bag to decorate the muffins with the icing. Optionally, decorate with chopped peanuts and grated chocolate.

Chocolate Cookies

Easy-to-make cookies in an instant. Whole cane sugar (not to be confused with raw sugar) is critical for its aroma. This sugar is made from the juice of sugar cane including the molasses. Unlike almost all other kinds of sugar, because whole cane sugar is unrefined, it contains many nutrients, particularly calcium, magnesium and iron.

Makes about 12
Difficulty *
Preparation time: 15 minutes plus
    12–14 minutes baking time

150 g/1¼ cups light wheat or spelt flour
⅓ tsp Bourbon vanilla powder
¾ tsp salt
60 g/generous ¼ cup sugar
60 g/generous ¼ cup whole cane sugar
25 g/¼ cup lightly defatted cocoa
    powder
90 g/7 tbsp vegan margarine
1 tbsp plant-based milk of your choice

Preheat the oven to 200°C/400°F.

Mix the dry ingredients in a bowl. Add the margarine and milk and knead well to form a compact dough ball. This takes some time, so keep kneading patiently until the dough no longer feels wet.

Shape the dough into 12 mounds and space them out evenly over a baking tray lined with baking parchment with sufficient space around them. Press lightly with a fork to give the cookies their typical texture. Don't press too hard; the cookies should be about 1 cm/½ in thick before baking. Bake for 12–14 minutes.

Chocolate Chip Cookies

Makes about 12
Difficulty *
Preparation time: 10 minutes plus
    8–12 minutes baking time

150 g/1¼ cups light wheat or spelt flour
¾ tsp Bourbon vanilla powder
¾ tsp baking powder
¾ tsp salt
60 g/generous ¼ cup sugar (see tip)
60 g/generous ¼ cup whole cane sugar
80 g/3¼ oz vegan dark chocolate
    (45–55 % cocoa solids), chopped, or
    80 g/3¼ oz vegan chocolate chips
90 g/7 tbsp vegan margarine
1 tbsp plant-based milk of your choice

Preheat the oven to 200°C/400°F.

Combine the dry ingredients in a bowl and mix well. Add the margarine and milk and knead well to form a compact dough ball.

Shape the dough into 12 mounds and space them out evenly over a baking tray lined with baking parchment with sufficient space around them. Press lightly with a fork to give the cookies their typical texture. Don't press too hard; the cookies should be about 1 cm/½ in thick before baking.

Bake for 8-12 minutes. They should turn golden brown. Take care that they don't become too dark.

Tip

If you prefer more of a caramel flavour, you can replace the white sugar in this recipe with whole cane sugar.

Cakes, Tarts
and Cheesecakes

My Sachertorte 🍴

'If life gives you chocolate, make Sachertorte with it!' The perfect vegan Sachertorte.
I've been polishing this recipe like no other, and for so long.
Surprise yourself!

For one 22 cm/8¾ in diameter springform cake tin
Difficulty ✳✳
Preparation time: 35 minutes plus 45–60 minutes
    baking time and approx. 3½ hours resting time

For the cake:
185 g/6½ oz vegan dark chocolate (45–55 % cocoa
    solids)
200 g/⅞ cup sugar
1 (9 g/0.32 oz) sachet vanilla sugar
200 g/scant 1 cup soft vegan margarine (leave out of
    the refrigerator for 1 hour to soften before use)
240 g/2 cups plus 2 tbsp light wheat flour
25 g/¼ cup cornflour
1 tbsp baking powder
¼ tsp salt
150 ml/⅔ cup water
2 tsp white wine vinegar
140 g/½ cup apricot jam

For the icing:
200 g/7 oz vegan dark chocolate (45–55 % cocoa
    solids)
90 g/7 tbsp vegan margarine

Preheat the oven to 180°C/350°F. Line the springform cake tin with baking parchment.

Slowly melt the chocolate over a bain-marie or in the microwave.

Combine the sugar, vanilla sugar and margarine in a bowl and beat until very fluffy. Fold in the melted chocolate.

Mix the flour, cornflour, baking powder and salt in a bowl. Add the flour mixture, water and vinegar to the chocolate mixture. Slowly and carefully fold together by hand with a scraper or in a food processor to a smooth batter. Do not mix too vigorously.

Pour the batter into the prepared cake tin and place on a shelf positioned on the second runner from the bottom. Bake for 45–60 minutes. Check that the cake is cooked through by pricking with a wooden or metal skewer. It should come out clean when you pull it out. Note: don't do this until the cake has been baking for at least 45 minutes, otherwise it may sink.

Turn off the oven and allow the cake to rest inside with the door slightly ajar for 30–40 minutes. The cake may sink a little. If this should happen, it can be fixed with icing. Unmould the cake, cover it completely with aluminium foil and leave to cool for at least 3 hours.

Use a large, sharp knife or a thin plastic thread or metal wire to carefully cut through the cake at one third of its height. Use two long knives or two rubber scrapers to carefully lift off the top and set it aside.

Spread 90 g/⅓ cup of jam over the bottom, and then gently replace the top part. Spread the rest of the jam over the top of the cake.

For the icing, slowly melt the chocolate with the margarine over a bain-marie or in the microwave. Use a brush or palette knife to spread the icing evenly over the top and sides of the cake. Leave to cool completely. (Picture on p. 46)

Tip

After cooling, cover the cake well with aluminium foil so that it doesn't dry out. If stored in the refrigerator – this is absolutely unnecessary – take it out 1½ hours before serving.

5-Minute Microwave Mug Cakes

Nothing could be simpler or quicker.
In 5 minutes you'll have a delicious chocolate cake.
These cakes are best enjoyed while they're still warm.

For a medium mug
Difficulty ✳
Preparation time: 5 minutes

65 g/9 tbsp light wheat or spelt flour
1½ tbsp sugar
2 tsp lightly defatted cocoa powder
1 large pinch Bourbon vanilla powder
¾ tsp baking powder
1 pinch salt
1½ tsp desiccated coconut (optional)
3 tbsp neutral sunflower or rapeseed oil
½ tsp white wine vinegar

Mix all the dry ingredients in a small bowl. Add 75 ml/⅓ cup of water, the vinegar and oil, and mix to a smooth batter. Transfer the batter to a mug of sufficient size. Bear in mind that the cake will roughly double in size in the microwave.

Put the mug in the microwave and cook for 2–3 minutes on a medium–high setting. The cooking time can vary depending on the microwave, so you'll need to pay attention the first time. The bottom of the cake should be pleasantly moist, not hard. (Picture on p. 47)

My Sachertorte

5-Minute Microwave Mug Cake

Saffron Cream Pie with a Biscuit Base

A biscuit base is a great alternative to the conventional pastry crust.
It stays fresher longer and goes wonderfully well with creamy fillings.
The little extra effort – you can even make the biscuits yourself – is definitely worthwhile.
The wonderful saffron cream ranks among my greatest achievements.

For one 24 cm/9½ in diameter springform
    cake tin
Difficulty ✷✷
Preparation time: 15 minutes plus
    8–10 minutes baking time

For the pie crust:
1 portion chocolate chip cookies (see
    recipe p. 40, or 350 g/12 oz chocolate
    cookies)
40 g/3 tbsp vegan margarine, room
    temperature or melted

For the cream:
175 ml/¾ cup soya milk (the high protein
    content is important, so no other plant-
    based milk can be used)
115 g/½ cup refined coconut oil, melted
70 g/¼ cup plus 2 tbsp sugar
1 medium lemon, for juice (about 50 ml/¼
    cup)
1 large pinch saffron threads
4–5 (10 g/ 0.35 oz) sachets whipped cream
    stabiliser
½ tsp salt

Preheat the oven to 200°C/400°F. Line the springform cake tin with baking parchment.

Finely crush the cookies with a rolling pin or in a food chopper. Add the margarine and 1–2 tablespoons of water and knead well until it forms a cohesive dough-like ball. Spread the biscuit base evenly over the prepared cake tin and bake for 8-10 minutes. Take the pie crust out of the oven and leave to cool for a short time.

Combine all the ingredients for the cream and mix well for 2–3 minutes with an electric hand mixer. Spread the cream out evenly over the slightly cooled pie crust. Refrigerate for at least 2 hours for the flavour to develop. Serve cold.

Tip

For a particularly decorative effect, scatter saffron threads over the pie.

Death by Chocolate

The ultimate chocolate cake! Along with the chocolate sushi, this is probably the most elaborate recipe in the book, but for all chocolate junkies – I don't hesitate to count myself as one – this will make your chocolate dreams come true.

For one 24 cm/9½ in sided square springform cake tin
    at least 5 cm/2 in deep (alternatively, use a 26
    cm/10¼ in diameter round tin)
Difficulty ✳✳✳
Preparation time: 1 hour plus 35–45 minutes baking
    time and at least 4½ hours resting time

For the cake batter:
300 g/1¼ cups soft vegan margarine (leave out of the
    refrigerator for 1 hour to soften before use)
300 g/1¼ cups sugar
40 g/⅓ cup cornflour
200 ml/scant 1 cup cold soya milk
240 g/2 cups plus 2 tbsp light wheat or spelt flour
90 g/¾ cup lightly defatted cocoa powder
1 tbsp baking powder
1 large pinch salt
The seeds from 1 vanilla pod
2 tsp white wine vinegar

For the icing:
200 g/7 oz vegan dark chocolate
    (45–55 % cocoa solids)
90 g/7 tbsp vegan margarine

For the cream filling:
200 g/7 oz vegan dark chocolate (45–55 % cocoa
    solids)
200 g/1 cup natural soya yoghurt, either sweetened
    or unsweetened

50 g/2 oz vegan white chocolate, grated (optional)

Preheat the oven to 180°C/350°F. Line the springform cake tin with baking parchment.

For the batter, beat the margarine with the sugar in a large bowl until fluffy.

Combine the flour, cocoa powder, baking powder, salt and vanilla seeds in a bowl, and mix well. Dissolve the cornflour completely in the cold soya milk. Add the flour mixture, soya milk and vinegar to the sugar and margarine mixture and carefully mix to a smooth batter. If the batter is too dry, add a 1–3 more tablespoons of soya milk.

Pour the batter into the cake tin and smooth the surface. Bake for 35–45 minutes. Check that the cake is cooked by pricking with a wooden skewer. If it doesn't come out clean, bake for a little longer. After baking, turn off the oven and allow the cake to rest inside with the door slightly ajar for 30–40 minutes.

In the meantime, make the icing. Slowly melt the chocolate with the margarine over a bain-marie or in the microwave. Take the cake out of the oven, but leave it in the tin. Pour the icing over the cake and spread over the top evenly. Leave to cool for a short while, and then cover the cake in the tin with aluminium foil and refrigerate for at least 2 hours (better longer).

Chocolate Cake – The Classic 🍫

The classic: super easy and quick to make, and always popular.

For the cream filling, slowly melt the chocolate over a bain-marie or in the microwave. Immediately stir the chocolate into the yoghurt to obtain a smooth cream. Leave to cool.

After cooling the cake, remove the springform tin. Use a sharp knife to cut the cake into about 10 rectangular pieces, and then cut the pieces in half through the middle. Carefully take off the tops and set aside. Spread the cream over the bottoms and carefully replace the tops. Cover well with foil and refrigerate again for at least 2 hours.

Take out of the refrigetor 1 hour before serving. Decorate with grated vegan white chocolate if you like.
(Picture on p. 52)

For one 900 g/2 lb loaf tin
Difficulty ✳
Preparation time: 15 minutes plus
      about 50 minutes baking time

225 g/1 cup sugar
210 g/1¾ cups light wheat flour
1 tbsp baking powder
2 pinches salt
75 g/⅔ cup lightly defatted cocoa
      powder
1½ tbsp cornflour
175 ml/¾ cup cold water
150 ml/⅔ cup neutral sunflower or rape
      seed oil
1 tsp white wine vinegar

Preheat the oven to 180°C/350°F. Line the loaf tin with baking parchment.

Mix the sugar, flour, baking powder, salt and cocoa powder in a bowl.

Dissolve the cornflour completely in cold water. Add the cornflour, oil and vinegar to the flour mixture and stir briskly with a tablespoon to a smooth batter.

Pour the batter into the tin and smooth the surface. Bake for about 50 minutes. Check that the cake is cooked through by pricking with a wooden or metal skewer. It should come out clean when you pull it out.
(Picture on p. 53)

Death by Chocolate

Chocolate Cake – The Classic

Chocolate Orange Marble Cake

For one 900 g/2 lb loaf tin

Difficulty *

Preparation time: 20 minutes plus
    55–65 minutes baking time

1–2 large, untreated orange(s), for grated
    zest and juice

250 g/1⅛ cup soft vegan margarine

125 g/generous ½ cup sugar

1 large pinch salt

290 g/2½ cups light wheat or spelt flour

1 tbsp baking powder

25 g/¼ cup lightly defatted cocoa powder

50 g/2 oz vegan dark chocolate (45–55 %
    cocoa solids), finely grated (optional)

100 g/generous ¾ cup icing sugar

Preheat the oven to 180°C/350°F. Line the loaf tin with baking parchment.

Rinse 1 orange under hot water and dry. Completely grate the zest and set aside. Squeeze the juice and set aside. The second orange will be used only if more juice is needed.

Beat the margarine with the sugar and salt in a bowl until fluffy. Mix the flour and baking powder, then add with the orange juice to the sugar and margarine mixture. Mix well to obtain a smooth batter.

Halve the batter. Stir the grated orange zest to one half of the batter. Add the cocoa powder, 4–5 tablespoons of water and the grated chocolate, if required, to the other half and mix until smooth.

Pour the light batter into the bottom of the loaf tin and smooth the surface. Spread the dark batter evenly over the top. Drag a fork through the batter to create the typical marble patterns.

Bake for 55–65 minutes. Check that the cake is cooked through by pricking with a wooden or metal skewer. It should come out clean when you pull it out.

For the icing, mix the icing sugar with 2 tablespoons of orange juice. The icing should be quite thick and definitely not too thin, so be careful when adding the orange juice. Spread the icing over the still warm cake, and then leave to cool completely.

Swedish Coffee Cake

Coconut and coffee meet chocolate in this Swedish cake.
Super easy to make and a real treat to have with a coffee or cappuccino.

For one 23 cm/9 in diameter springform cake tin
Difficulty ✳
Preparation time: 20 minutes plus
    35–40 minutes baking time and 40 minutes
    resting time

For the cake batter:
210 g/1¾ cups light wheat or spelt flour
200 g/⅞ cup sugar
1 tbsp baking powder
25 g/¼ cup lightly defatted cocoa powder
1 (9 g/ 0.32 oz) sachet vanilla sugar
1 pinch salt
100 ml/scant ½ cup neutral vegetable oil
200 ml/scant 1 cup soya milk or almond milk
2 tsp white wine vinegar

For the icing:
75 g/6 tbsp vegan margarine, melted
160 g/generous 1¼ cups sifted icing sugar
¾ tsp vanilla sugar
1 tbsp lightly defatted cocoa powder
1 tsp instant coffee dissolved in 4 tbsp hot water
    (or 4 tbsp very strong coffee, eg espresso)

50–100 g/½–1 cup desiccated coconut for
    sprinkling

Preheat the oven to 190°C/375°F. Line the springform cake tin with baking parchment.

For the batter, combine the dry ingredients in a bowl and mix well. Add the oil, soya milk and vinegar, and mix until smooth. Pour the batter into the tin and smooth the surface. Bake for about 35–40 minutes (check that it is cooked through by pricking with a skewer). Leave the cake to cool for 20 minutes in the tin, then remove the tin.

In the meantime, combine the ingredients for the icing and mix well, preferably with a whisk. Shortly before use, heat the icing in a saucepan to leave it nice and runny. Cover the cake completely with the runny icing, allowing it to run down the sides of the cake to form a nice crust. Then put the springform tin back on the cake. If you don't want to cover the sides with icing, you can ice the cake once it is back in the tin.

Leave the icing for 20 minutes to harden, then sprinkle generously with desiccated coconut. Remove the springform pan.

Tip

The cake tastes even better the next day when some of the icing has been absorbed by the cake and a nice crust has formed.

Healthy Lifestyle Chocolate and Orange Tart

This tart is a real treat, and especially refreshing in summer. It needs to be kept in the freezer and should be taken out shortly before serving to allow it to thaw a little.

The chocolate literally melts in the mouth, a dream for everybody who – like myself – loves the combination of chocolate and orange.

For one 28 cm/11 in diameter springform cake tin
Difficulty ∗∗
Preparation time: 30 minutes plus 3 hours
   freezing time

For the tart base:
175 g/1 cup pitted dates, as soft as possible
   (pitted weight, see tip on p. 60)
150 g ground almonds
50 g ground hazelnuts
75 g/6 tbsp refined coconut oil, melted

For the caramel filling:
220 g /1¼ cups pitted soft Medjool dates (pitted
   weight, see tip on p. 60) or other soft dates
⅓ tsp sea salt
1 heaped tbsp concentrated pear juice or maple
   syrup

For the chocolate cream:
40 g/⅓ cup lightly defatted cocoa powder
75 g/6 tbsp refined coconut oil, melted
1 tbsp concentrated pear juice or maple syrup
30 ml/2 tbsp agave syrup or 25 g/¼ cup sifted
   icing sugar
2 untreated oranges for grated zest and juice
   (total 200 ml/scant 1 cup)
25 g/2 tbsp white almond butter

Line the springform cake tin with baking parchment.

Finely chop the dates for the base. Mix with the ground almonds, hazelnuts, 1½ tablespoons of water and the melted coconut oil. Knead vigorously to obtain a dough. Spread the dough evenly over the bottom of the prepared cake tin and press firmly to leave a 1 cm/½ in border around the sides.

For the caramel filling, combine the dates with 250 ml/1 cup of water, the salt and concentrated pear syrup in a deep container, and blend with a hand-held blender until you have a smooth cream without any lumps. Spread the cream over the tart base. Place in the freezer for at least 1 hour.

In the meantime, make the chocolate cream. Combine all the ingredients in a bowl and blend well. After the caramel layer has frozen, take the tart base out of the freezer and spread the chocolate cream over it. Return the tart to the freezer for at least another 2 hours.

Healthy Lifestyle Chocolate Cheesecake

So delicious and so healthy! This cheesecake can be made in a 26 cm/10¼ in diameter springform cake tin with double the given measures.

For one 16 cm/6¼ in square cake tin or an
    18 cm/7 in diameter springform cake tin
Difficulty ✳✳
Preparation time: 40 minutes plus 6 hours
    freezing time and a few hours refrigeration
    time

For the base:
60 g/⅓ cup pitted dates, as soft as possible
    (pitted weight, see tip)
25 g/¼ cup cocoa powder
60 g/½ cup ground hazelnuts
25 g/2 tbsp refined coconut oil, melted

For the filling:
1 medium banana
200 g/1¾ cups cashew nuts (see tip)
75 g/scant ½ cup pitted dates, as soft as
    possible (pitted weight, see tip)
1 tbsp lemon juice
40 g/⅓ cup cocoa powder
¾ tsp Bourbon-vanilla powder or the seeds
    from ½ vanilla pod
1 pinch salt
25–40 g/2–3 tbsp refined coconut oil, melted

The banana for the filling should be ripe enough to smell through the skin, but not overripe. Peel and slice the banana, and freeze for at least 6 hours.

Line the cake tin with baking parchment.

For the base, slice the dates finely with a knife. Mix with the cocoa powder and ground hazelnuts in a bowl. Add 2 teaspoons of water and the coconut oil, and knead vigorously to a dough. Spread the dough over the bottom of the cake tin.

For the filling, take the banana out of the freezer and leave to thaw slightly. Combine with the cashews, dates, lemon juice and 5 tablespoons of water in a blender and blend to a smooth cream. If necessary, you can also let the banana thaw out a little more and purée it with a hand-held blender.

Mix in the cocoa powder, vanilla, salt and melted coconut oil, and spread the mixture over the base. Refrigerate for a few hours so that it becomes firm.

Tips

You can buy dates that are already soft. As a suitable alternative, Medjool dates are naturally soft.

If the cashews are soaked overnight in water, the amount of water required for the filling can be reduced by 1–2 tablespoons.

Chocolate Cheesecake

For a not so healthy lifestyle.

For one 18 cm/7 in diameter springform
    cake tin
Difficulty ✱✱
Preparation time: 30 minutes plus 12 hours
    draining time, 1 hour baking time and
    1½ hours refrigeration time

For the pastry:
125 g/generous 1 cup light wheat or spelt
    flour
1 pinch salt
1 tbsp sugar
60 g/5 tbsp vegan margarine

For the filling:
500 g/2½ cups natural soya yoghurt,
    unsweetened (see tip)
100 ml/scant ½ cup soya milk
1½ tbsp lemon juice
40 g/⅓ cup cornflour
130 g/9 tbsp vegan margarine, melted
100 g/⅜ cup sugar
2 tbsp concentrated pear juice or maple
    syrup
25 g/¼ cup lightly defatted cocoa powder
½ tsp Bourbon vanilla powder
1 pinch salt
2 tbsp rum (optional)

Leave the yoghurt to drain overnight in a sieve lined with 2 layers of kitchen paper.

The next day, make the pastry by mixing the flour with the salt and sugar. Knead in the margarine with your fingers until no lumps can be felt.

Add 2 tablespoons of water and knead a little longer. Refrigerate for at least 30 minutes.

Preheat the oven to 180°C/350°F. Line the springform cake tin with baking parchment.

Spread the dough evenly over the bottom of the prepared cake tin and bake for 10 minutes.

In the meantime, make the filling by mixing the soya milk with the lemon juice and cornflour. Transfer the drained yoghurt to a bowl.

Add the soya milk mixture and the other ingredients for the filling. Mix well with a whisk to obtain a nice, creamy, lump-free mixture. Spread the filling over the pre-baked pastry base.

Raise the oven temperature to 190°C/375°F and bake the cheesecake for 50 minutes. Leave to cool, and then refrigerate for at least 1 hour.

Tip
Sweetened soya yoghurt can naturally be used for the filling, but the sugar in the recipe will have to be reduced to 70 g/¼ cup plus 2 tbsp.

Berry Pie with a Chocolate Crust

For one 28 cm/11 in diameter round baking tin
Difficulty ✳
Preparation time: 20 minutes plus about 30
minutes refrigeration and the same for
baking

For the pastry:
240 g/2 cups plus 2 tbsp light wheat or spelt
flour
½ tsp salt
3 tbsp sugar
25 g/¼ cup lightly defatted cocoa powder
50 g/2 oz vegan dark chocolate (45–55 % cocoa
solids), grated
90 g/7 tbsp vegan margarine
1 tsp white wine vinegar

For the glaze:
300 ml/1¼ cups almond or soya milk
40 g/3 tbsp white almond butter
The seeds from 1 vanilla pod or
⅓ tsp Bourbon vanilla powder
2½ tbsp freshly squeezed lemon juice
70 g/¼ cup plus 2 tbsp sugar
2 tbsp cornflour
1 pinch salt

For the filling:
5 tbsp ground almonds
500 g/4 cups assorted frozen berries
(raspberries, blackberries, redcurrants,
strawberries)
5 tbsp raspberry or blackberry jam

Preheat the oven to 220°C/425°F.

For the pastry, combine the flour, salt, sugar, cocoa powder and grated chocolate in a bowl, and mix well. Add the margarine and work it in with your fingers, without kneading, until no lumps can be felt.

Mix the vinegar and 100 ml/scant ½ cup of cold water and add it to the dough. Briefly knead, roll the dough into a compact ball, cover with aluminium foil and refrigerate for at least 30 minutes.

Combine all the ingredients for the glaze and blend well with an electric hand mixer.

Grease the baking tin and spread the pastry over evenly. Spread the ground almonds out over the pastry base. Prick the pastry repeatedly with a fork. Cover the pastry with the berries, then spread the jam over the top. Finally, cover with an even layer of glaze. Place the pie on a shelf positioned on the second runner from the bottom. Bake for 30–35 minutes.

Chocoholic Favourites

Chocoholic Custard Slices

Traditional millefeuille pastries filled with vanilla custard, are a Swiss classic.
But honestly, who needs vanilla? This chocolate version will knock your socks off!

Makes 6
Difficulty ✷✷
Preparation time: 40 minutes plus
    12–15 minutes baking time

1 rectangular sheet vegan puff pastry
    (320 g; 36 x 24 cm/14¼ x 9½ in)

For the filling:
75 g/3 oz vegan dark chocolate (45–55 %
    cocoa solids)
300 ml/1¼ cups soya whipping cream
1½–2 (10 g/0.35 oz) sachets whipped cream
    stabiliser
3 tbsp sugar
¼ tsp Bourbon vanilla powder
1 pinch salt
25 g/1 oz vegan dark chocolate (45–55 %
    cocoa solids), grated, or 25 g/1 oz
    vegan chocolate sprinkles

For the topping:
60 g/¼ cup apricot jam
100 g/3¾ oz vegan dark chocolate (45–55 %
    cocoa solids)
50 g/¼ cup vegan margarine

Preheat the oven to 200°C/400°F.

Roll out the puff pastry over a baking tray lined with baking parchment, and trim to the required size. Prick the pastry repeatedly with a fork so that it rises as little as possible. Cut the pastry across its width to make 3 uniform 12 x 24 cm/4½ x 9½ in strips. Bake for 12–15 minutes until light golden.

For the chocolate filling, slowly melt the chocolate over a bain-marie or in the microwave. Whip the soya cream for 1–2 minutes with an electric hand mixer. Sprinkle in the stabiliser and whip for another 2 minutes until the cream is firm. Depending on the cream you use, you may need more or less stabiliser.

Fold the melted chocolate, sugar, vanilla and salt into the whipped cream to make a nice chocolate mousse. Finally, gently fold the grated chocolate or chocolate sprinkles into the mousse.

The mousse must be firm, otherwise refrigerate for 1 or 2 hours.

Spread half of the mousse over one of the three pastry strips, right to the edge. Take the second strip, place it over the first and spread the other half of the mousse over it. Finally cover with the last strip, with the smooth side facing upwards.

For the topping, lightly warm the apricot jam and carefully brush over the top of the pastry. Slowly melt the chocolate with the margarine over a bain-marie or in the microwave, and spread this icing over the top of the pastry. Don't spread this icing right to the edges as none of it should cover the sides. Wait until the chocolate has firmed a little, but still remaining soft, then use a brush to spread the icing to the edges.

Use a sharp serrated knife to cut the pastry into six 12 x 4 cm/4½ x 1½ in slices. Allow to cool fully. Best served cold.

Super Easy Chocolate Croissants

Makes 8–10

Difficulty ✳

Preparation time: 10 minutes plus
14–20 minutes baking time

150 g/5 oz vegan dark chocolate (45–55 %
cocoa solids)

1 round sheet vegan puff pastry (275 g/8 oz,
32 cm/12½ in in diameter), very cold

1 tsp plant-based cream with ½ tsp ground
turmeric (optional)

Use a sharp knife to chop 100 g/3¾ oz of the chocolate into very small pieces.

Cut the pastry into 8–10 uniform segments (like slices of a pie), depending on the size of the croissants. Note: the pastry should be refrigerated for at least 2 hours before use, and can be used directly from the refrigerator.

Preheat the oven to 220°C/425°F.

Place 1–1½ teaspoons of chopped chocolate in the middle of each piece of puff pastry, about ½ cm/¼ in from the bottom edge. Carefully roll them up from the bottom edge towards the tip. Push the sides in and press lightly. Bend slightly into a crescent – the typical croissant shape. Lay the croissants over a baking tray lined with parchment paper.

Optionally, you can brush a little cream with turmeric lightly over the croissants. Place the baking tray in the oven and position an oven shelf in the runner immediately above it to stop the pastry rising too much. Bake the croissants for 14-20 minutes until golden brown.

Melt the rest of the chocolate over a bain-marie or in the microwave, Brush the chocolate over both ends of the croissants or decorate the croissants with it as you please.

Tip

The croissants should be allowed to cool a little and are best served warm.

Crunchy Chocolate and Cinnamon Granola

Nothing beats home-made granola. This version has a particularly aromatic flavour.
The combination of cinnamon and chocolate is brought to full effect during baking.
Granola, accompanied by spelt or rice milk, is one of my favourite snacks.
Dry, it also makes a good snack to have on the go.

Makes 1 kg
Difficulty ✳✳
Preparation time: 15 minutes plus 35
    minutes baking time and 3–4
    hours resting time

2 x 125 g/generous 1 cup coarse
    oatmeal
2 x 125 g/generous 1 cup pinhead
    oatmeal
2 x 40 g/½ cup puffed oats
2 x 25 g/¼ cup desiccated coconut
2 x ⅔ tsp ground cinnamon
2 x ⅓ tsp Bourbon vanilla powder
65 g/9 tbsp lightly defatted cocoa
    powder
75–120 ml/⅓–½ cup concentrated
    pear juice or maple syrup,
    depending on the desired
    sweetness
100 ml/scant ½ cup neutral vegetable
    oil
Sultanas and corn flakes (as needed)

Combine each portion of the coarse and pinhead
oatmeal, puffed oats, desiccated coconut, cinnamon
and vanilla, respectively in two separate bowls and mix
well. Add the cocoa powder to one of the bowls and
mix well.

Heat the concentrated pear juice, oil and 120 ml/
scant ½ cup of water in a saucepan. Bring to the boil,
then pour equal amounts in to both bowls. Make sure
that the oil floating on the surface doesn't get poured
into only one of the bowls. Now mix until the liquid is
as evenly distributed as possible.

Combine both mixtures and spread over a baking
tray. Place in a cold oven. Set the temperature to
180°C/350°F and bake for 35 minutes. Stir the mixture
after 25 minutes. After baking, turn off the oven. Leave
the granola in the still warm oven with the door closed
for 3–4 hours. This step will produce a particularly
even crispiness.

Take the granola out of the oven and mix with
sultanas and corn flakes.

Tip

You can also make up double the measures of this
recipe. Simply spread it out over two baking trays and
bake one at the top and the other at the bottom of the
oven.

NB

Because they contain very little gluten compared to
other cereals, oats are relatively well tolerated by
people affected by coeliac disease, when consumed in
moderate amounts. When shopping, it is absolutely
essential to look out for special gluten-free oat
products that haven't been contaminated with gluten
from other products. However, people who are allergic
to avenin, a protein present in oats, should totally
avoid oats and oat products.

Gingerbread Mousse Tartlets

Makes 7–9

Difficulty *

Preparation time: 25 minutes plus at least 1½ hours
    refrigeration time and 15–17 minutes
    baking time

For the mousse:

200 ml/scant 1 cup soya whipping cream,
    unsweetened (see tip)

1 (9 g/0.32 oz) sachet whipped cream stabiliser

40 g/1½ oz vegan dark chocolate
    (45–55 % cocoa solids)

1 tsp gingerbread spice blend

1–1½ tbsp maple syrup (grade A)

1 pinch salt

1 tbsp rum or 2 drops rum flavouring (optional)

Cocoa powder for sprinkling

For the tartlet cases:

150 g/1¼ cups light wheat flour

1½ tbsp sugar

1 pinch salt

75 g/6 tbsp cold vegan margarine

Preheat the oven to 200°C/400°F.

For the mousse, whip the cream with an electric hand mixer on high speed. Sprinkle in the stabiliser and whip for another 2 minutes.

Slowly melt the chocolate over a bain-marie or in the microwave. Add the gingerbread spice, maple syrup, salt, 2 tablespoons of the whipped cream and, optionally, the rum or rum flavouring, and mix to a smooth cream. Carefully fold the cream into the remaining whipped cream to obtain a smooth mousse. Refrigerate the mousse for at least 1 hour, although preferably for 2–3 hours.

For the tartlet cases, mix the flour with the sugar and salt. Add the margarine and work it in with your fingers, without kneading, until there are no more lumps. Add 50 ml/¼ cup of water, knead briefly and roll into a compact ball. Wrap in aluminium foil and refrigerate for at least 30 minutes.

Grease 7–9 tartlet moulds (or the cavities of a muffin mould) and line each one with the pastry, leaving a border of 1–1½ cm/½–⅝ in around the sides. Prick the pastry repeatedly with a fork, and then bake for 15–17 minutes. Leave to cool. Fill a piping bag with the mousse and pipe a uniform amount into the cooled tartlet cases. Before serving, dust with cocoa powder. Store the mousse-filled tartlets in the refrigerator until it is time to serve.

Tip

If you prefer to use a sweetened plant-based whipping cream, simply reduce the amount of maple syrup to 2–3 teaspoons.

Pear and Chocolate Gratin
with Hazelnut Streusel

Serves 4

Difficulty *

Preparation time: 20 minutes plus
   35–40 minutes baking time

For the gratin:

450 g/1 lb ripe pears

375 ml/generous 1½ cups soya milk

2 tbsp cornflour

25 g/¼ cup lightly defatted cocoa powder

40 g/3 tbsp hazelnut butter or brown almond butter

60 g/generous ¼ cup sugar

1 pinch salt

1½ tsp vanilla sugar

1 tbsp freshly squeezed lemon juice

For the streusel:

60 g/½ cup ground hazelnuts

1½ tsp sugar

2–3 tsp lemon juice

1 tsp grated lemon zest (untreated lemon)

Preheat the oven to 200°C/400°F.

Wash, core and slice the pears. Arrange the pear slices in a large, greased gratin dish or divide evenly between several smaller moulds.

Combine the remaining ingredients for the gratin and mix well with an electric hand mixer to a smooth sauce.

For the streusel, mix the ground hazelnuts with the sugar. Add the lemon juice and grated zest and knead vigorously with your fingers. The streusel should not be moist, nor should it be too dry. Adjust the amount of lemon juice accordingly.

Pour the sauce over the pears, put the dish in the oven and bake for 35–40 minutes.

After baking for 20 minutes, take the gratin out of the oven and crumble the streusel over the top. Return the dish to the oven and finish baking. The streusel should turn golden brown.

Marzipan and Chocolate Bar 🍫

Makes 8–10

Difficulty **

Preparation time: 20 minutes plus at least 30
    minutes cooling time and 20 minutes
    baking time

For the biscuit:

100 g/generous ¾ cup light wheat or spelt flour

¼ tsp baking powder

45 g/scant ¼ cup sugar

2 pinches salt

75 g/6 tbsp vegan margarine

For the filling and coating:

375 g/13 oz soft marzipan

100 g/3¾ oz vegan dark chocolate (45–55 %
    cocoa solids)

20 g/1½ tbsp vegan margarine

Preheat the oven to 200°C/400°F.

For the biscuit, combine the flour, baking powder, sugar and salt, and mix well. Add the margarine and work in with your fingers. Add 4 teaspoons of water, knead vigorously for a short time, and then roll the dough into a ball. If the dough is very dry, add another teaspoon of water. It should be moist but not wet. Wrap the dough in aluminium foil and refrigerate for at least 30 minutes.

Halve the dough and roll each half out on a sheet of baking parchment under a sheet of cling film to make two rectangles measuring 26 x 10 cm/10¼ x 4 in. Trim with a knife if necessary. Bake for 20 minutes, and then leave to cool.

Use a sharp knife to cut the rectangles across their width to make 8–10 bars.

Roll out the marzipan and cut into pieces the same size as the bars and place them over the biscuit base. Take care that the marzipan doesn't break.

For the coating, slowly melt the chocolate with the margarine over a bain-marie and brush it over the bars.

Chocolate Biscuit Slices
with Lemon 'Cream Cheese' Filling

Makes 6

Difficulty **

Preparation time: 25 minutes plus 10 minutes
baking time and 4 hours cooling time

For the biscuit:

100 g/generous ¾ cup light wheat or spelt flour

1 (9 g/0.32 oz) sachet vanilla sugar

1 (9 g/0.32 oz) sachet baking powder

2 tbsp lightly defatted cocoa powder

2 tbsp cornflour

70 g/¼ cup plus 2 tbsp sugar

1 pinch salt

1 tsp white wine vinegar

120 ml/½ cup soya milk

2 tbsp neutral vegetable oil

Fat/oil for greasing

For the cream:

120 ml/½ cup soya milk (the high protein
content is important, so no other plant-
based milk can be used)

75 g/6 tbsp refined coconut oil, melted

50 g/¼ cup sugar

½ untreated lemon, for grated zest

60 ml/4 tbsp freshly squeezed lemon juice

4 (10 g/0.35 oz) sachets whipped cream
stabiliser

1 pinch salt

Preheat the oven to 200°C/400°F.

For the biscuit, combine the dry ingredients in a bowl and mix well. Add the vinegar, soya milk and oil, and mix well. Spread the wet dough out over a greased baking tray into a 24 cm/9½ in square. Bake for 10 minutes, and then leave to cool. Cut the biscuit lengthways into two 12 cm/4½ in wide strips. Cut each of the halves into six 4 x 12 cm/1½ x 4½ in strips.

For the cream, combine all the ingredients and mix well for 2–3 minutes with an electric hand mixer. Refrigerate for at least 4 hours.

Spread about 1 tablespoon of the cream over the porous side of one strip and cover with a second strip. These slices will keep for about 2–3 days in the refrigerator covered in aluminium foil.

Chocolate Yeast Rolls 🐻

There's nothing like a fresh chocolate roll! With this recipe you can get everybody out of bed as soon as the smell of baking bread comes wafting from the oven.

Makes 8

Difficulty **

Preparation time: 30 minutes plus 45–60 minutes proving time and 15–18 minutes baking time

20 g/¾ oz fresh yeast

1 tsp plus 1 tbsp sugar

100 ml/scant ½ cup lukewarm almond milk or soya milk

210 g/1¾ cups light wheat or spelt flour

¼ tsp salt

2 tbsp desiccated coconut (optional)

50 g/¼ cup soft vegan margarine

Version 1: Vegan Nutella (see recipe on p. 18) or another chocolate spread

Version 2: 75 g/3 oz vegan chocolate chips or 75 g/3 oz vegan dark chocolate, finely chopped

Pearl sugar (optional, as needed)

Fully dissolve the yeast and 1 teaspoon of sugar in the lukewarm almond milk.

Combine the flour with 1 tablespoon of sugar, the salt and, optionally, the desiccated coconut, and mix well. Add the yeast mixture and the soft margarine, and knead vigorously for 10 minutes to a smooth dough. Transfer the dough to a bowl, cover with a cloth and leave to prove in a warm place (at least 22°C/72°F, maximum 50°C/122°F) for 45–60 minutes until it doubles in size.

Preheat the oven to 200°C/400°F.

Divide the dough into 8 uniform balls and place them on a baking tray lined with baking parchment.

For version 1, press the balls flat and place 1 generous teaspoon of vegan Nutella in the middle. Fold up the sides of the dough to the middle and seal the well, so that the filling doesn't leak out when baked. Turn the rolls over so that the join is resting on the tray.

For version 2, knead the chocolate chips or finely chopped chocolate into the dough.

You can prove the dough balls again if you like, so that they become especially fluffy. But if you'd rather not wait, you can put them straight into the oven and bake for 15–18 minutes, until they turn golden. You can also decorate them with pearl sugar. Best served a little warm.

Chocolate Focaccia
with Rosemary and Sea Salt 🍫

This focaccia has a light but not overpowering chocolate flavour that makes it a culinary treat when combined with salty and savoury food.

Makes 1 focaccia
Difficulty ✳✳
Preparation time: 10 minutes plus 1–1½ hours proving time and 22–25 minutes baking time

20 g/¾ oz fresh yeast
1 tsp sugar
75 ml/⅓ cup lukewarm plant-based milk (preferably soya or almond milk)
100 g/3¾ oz vegan dark chocolate (45–55 % cocoa solids)
240 g/2 cups plus 2 tbsp light wheat or spelt flour
Sea salt
1 tbsp fresh rosemary, finely chopped
1 tbsp mild olive oil
Flour for the work surface

Fully dissolve the yeast and the sugar in the lukewarm milk.

Slowly melt the chocolate over a bain-marie or in the microwave.

Mix the flour with a pinch of salt and the chopped rosemary. Add the dissolved yeast, 50 ml/¼ cup of water, the melted chocolate and oil to the flour mixture and knead together vigorously until the dough no longer sticks.

Transfer the dough to a bowl, cover with a cloth and leave to prove – either at room temperature (ideally 22–35°C/72–95°F) for 1–1½ hours, or in a preheated oven at 50°C/112°F for 45 minutes – until it doubles in size.

Preheat the oven to 200°C/400°F.

Knead the dough again briefly, and then roll it out over a floured work surface to a 20 x 30 cm/8 x 12 in rectangle. Transfer to a baking tray lined with parchment paper. Use a knife to score the surface with a diamond pattern, and sprinkle with sea salt. Bake for 22–25 minutes.

No-Bake
Chocolate
Treats

My Bounties 🌾 🍫

These bars are one of my favourite sweet surprises.
I always have a portion stored away in my freezer to enjoy whenever I want, or to give away.

Makes 15–30, depending on size
Difficulty **
Preparation time: 30 minutes plus at least 2 hours
    cooling time

For the coconut mixture:
150 g/1½ cups desiccated coconut
¾ (9 g/0.32 oz) sachet vanilla sugar
70 g/¼ cup plus 2 tbsp sugar
1 pinch salt
75 g/6 tbsp refined coconut oil
75 ml/⅓ cup almond or soya milk
150 ml/⅔ cup coconut milk
1½ tbsp cornflour

For the coating:
185 g/6½ oz vegan dark chocolate (45–55 %
    cocoa solids)
50 g/¼ cup vegan margarine

Combine all the ingredients for the coconut mixture, except the cornflour, in a saucepan and heat slowly until the coconut oil is completely melted. Then stir in the cornflour. Leave the mixture to cool completely, then refrigerate for at least 1 hour to harden.

After refrigerating, stir the coconut mixture for a short time, and then use your hands to shape into very compact bars of the desired size. It's a good idea to refrigerate them again (if you're in a hurry, you can also use them as they are).

For the chocolate coating, slowly melt the chocolate and margarine completely over a bain-marie over a low heat. Use two teaspoons to dip the coconut bars in the chocolate and lay them on a sheet of baking parchment. Leave to cool completely. They should be allowed to harden again in the refrigerator.

Spiced Chocolate Mousse

Nutmeg, cloves and cinnamon – three spices which, together with cocoa and chocolate, call to mind the unforgettable flavour of **Magenbrot**, Swiss alpine gingerbread.
If you like **Magenbrot**, you'll love this mousse!

Serves 3–4

Difficulty *

Preparation time: 10 minutes plus at least 1 hour cooling time

400 ml/1⅔ cups soya whipping cream

2½-3 (10 g/0.35 oz) sachets whipped cream stabiliser

60 g/2¼ oz vegan dark chocolate (45–55 % cocoa solids)

2 tsp lightly defatted cocoa powder

⅓ tsp ground nutmeg

⅔ tsp ground cloves

1 tsp ground cinnamon

1 large pinch salt

50 ml/¼ cup concentrated pear juice, or concentrated apple juice or maple syrup

100 g/3¾ oz vegan *Magenbrot* (optional, see tips)

Whip the cream with an electric hand mixer for 2 minutes. Sprinkle in the stabiliser and whip for another 2 minutes.

Slowly melt the chocolate over a bain-marie. Add the cocoa powder, spices, salt and concentrated pear juice, and mix to a smooth cream. Add 2 tablespoons of the whipped cream and mix until smooth. Carefully fold this cream into the remaining whipped cream to obtain a smooth, fluffy mousse. Refrigerate the mousse for at least 1 hour, although preferably for 2–3 hours.

Optionally, you can crumble some **Magenbrot** with your fingers and sprinkle it over the mousse.

Tips

It's very important when following this recipe to be extremely precise when measuring out the spices. Even small deviations can mean that the spices will either be overpowering or unnoticeable.

You may find vegan **Magenbrot** in some supermarkets and organic food shops, or online.

Frozen Mocha and Chocolate Cream Tart with a Hazelnut and Date Crust 🌾 🥜

I've never really been into coffee as a drink, but coffee ice cream has always fascinated me. This frozen mocha tart is a real summer delight.

For one 18 cm/7 in diameter springform cake tin or another mould of a similar size but with high sides

Difficulty ✳✳

Preparation time: 20 minutes plus at least 3 hours cooling time

For the tart base:

100 g/generous ½ cup pitted soft dates (pitted weight, see tip)

90 g/¾ cup ground hazelnuts

½ tsp ground cinnamon

For the chocolate cream:

3 tbsp lightly defatted cocoa powder

3 tbsp neutral vegetable oil

3 tbsp maple syrup or concentrated pear juice

For the mocha filling:

2 tsp instant coffee powder

70 g/¼ cup plus 2 tbsp sugar

40 g/3 tbsp cashew butter or white almond butter

1 pinch salt

The seeds from ½ vanilla pod

4 tsp coffee beans

Coffee beans, cranberries and pistachios to decorate (optional, as needed)

For the tart base, chop the dates and knead together with the ground hazelnuts and cinnamon. If necessary, add teaspoons of water to make the dough easier to knead, but it shouldn't be too moist. Line the bottom of the tin with baking parchment and cover with the pastry.

For the chocolate cream, combine all the ingredients and mix to a smooth cream. Spread the cream over the tart base.

For the mocha filling, combine all the ingredients, except the coffee beans, in a saucepan with 300 ml/1¼ cups of water and bring to the boil to completely dissolve the sugar and coffee. Leave to cool for a short time. Grind the coffee beans in a food chopper and fold into the mocha cream. Pour this cream over the chocolate cream and spread smoothly.

Place the tart in the freezer for at least 3 hours. Keep it in the freezer until it is time to serve. Take it out of the freezer some 10–15 minutes before serving and allow it to thaw slightly. You can decorate it with coffee beans, cranberries and/or pistachios if you like.

Tip

Soft dates can be found in supermarkets. They're perfect for this recipe.

Alternatively, you can buy Medjool dates, which are naturally very soft and easy to work with.

Peanut Tartlets 🌾 🥜

If you love peanut and chocolate bars, you'll adore these tartlets.

Makes 12-14

Difficulty ✳

Preparation time: 15 minutes plus 3 hours
refrigeration time

For the peanut base:

75 g/6 tbsp refined coconut oil

150 g/10 tbsp peanut butter or 130 g/9 tbsp
peanut butter plus 20 g/1½ tbsp coconut oil

100 g/generous ¾ cup sifted icing sugar

The seeds from 1 vanilla pod

60 g/½ cup salted and roasted peanuts

¾ tsp salt

For the filling:

150 g/5 oz vegan dark chocolate (45–55 %
cocoa solids)

50 g/¼ cup peanut butter

For the peanut base, combine the coconut oil with the peanut butter in a saucepan and place over a low heat until both ingredients are fully melted. Add the icing sugar, vanilla seeds, peanuts and salt, and stir until the sugar is completely dissolved.

Spread the peanut mixture evenly to a height of 1 cm/½ in in 12–14 paper or silicone cupcake cases. Place the cases on a tray and refrigerate for 1 hour. If you're in a hurry, put them in the freezer for 30 minutes. Ideally, the peanut base shouldn't be too firm for the next step, but slightly runny.

For the filling, slowly melt the chocolate and peanut butter over a bain-marie and stir to a smooth cream. Pour a layer of chocolate cream over the peanut base in each cupcake case.

If the base is still runny, drag a fork once or twice across the base through the layers to create a pretty pattern. This is purely decorative and isn't a necessary step. Refrigerate for at least another 2 hours. The tartlets can be served directly from the refrigerator.

Tip

These tartlets will freeze very well, and they can be thawed and enjoyed at will.

Almond and Chocolate Panna Cotta with a Berry Sauce 🌾 🐝

Makes 4

Difficulty ✳

Preparation time: 20 minutes plus at least 1 hour
    cooling time

For the panna cotta:

400 ml/1⅔ cups water

25 g/2 tbsp white almond butter

40 g/1½ oz vegan dark chocolate
    (45–55 % cocoa solids)

¾ tsp Bourbon vanilla powder or the seeds from ½
    vanilla pod

45 g/scant ¼ cup sugar

2 tsp lemon juice

10 g/2 tsp brown almond butter (optional)

1 tsp agar-agar

For the berry sauce:

215 g/1¾ cups assorted frozen berries
    (blackberries, blueberries, raspberries,
    strawberries), thawed (with collected juice)

100 ml/scant ½ cup grape juice

2 tbsp sugar

For the panna cotta, combine the water, white almond butter, chocolate, vanilla, sugar, lemon juice and, optionally, the brown almond butter in a saucepan and bring to the boil. Simmer over a medium heat and stir with a whisk until the chocolate is completely melted. Sprinkle in the agar-agar and simmer for another 1–2 minutes while stirring constantly.

Fill four small glasses, cups or small plastic bowls and leave to cool, and then refrigerate for at least 1 hour.

For the sauce, combine the thawed berries, their juice, the grape juice and sugar in a saucepan and bring to the boil. Simmer over a medium heat for 2–3 minutes uncovered.

Unmould the panna cotta on plates and serve with the sauce.

Tip

If a panna cotta doesn't want to come out of its mould, it helps to dip the bowl halfway in hot water or, failing that, run a thin, sharp knife around the edge to loosen it, then it will slide out easily.

Grandma's Chocolate-Covered Dates

Chocolate-covered dates were my maternal grandmother's speciality, and they still remind me of Christmas as a child.

I took her recipe and developed it. Of course, the version I present here is vegan.

Dates are particularly used at Christmas to decorate biscuits and confectionery.

Makes 30

Difficulty ✳✳

Preparation time: 30 minutes

30 blanched almonds

1 tbsp concentrated pear juice or maple syrup

1 tsp gingerbread spice blend

30 dates (Deglet Nour variety, don't use very moist dates)

90 g/3½ oz vegan dark chocolate (45–55 % cocoa solids)

40 g/3 tbsp vegan margarine

grated vegan dark chocolate and/or vegan white chocolate (optional, as needed)

Roast the almonds in a dry non-stick frying pan on a high heat for 3–5 minutes, turning regularly, until they turn a light golden brown. On no account should they turn black. Remove the pan from the heat, and immediately add the concentrated pear juice and gingerbread spices. Mix well. Leave the almonds to stand in the pan off the heat for 1–2 minutes, and then transfer to a sheet of baking parchment. Spread the almonds out so that they don't stick to each other.

Make a slit in the dates and remove the stone, but do not cut completely in half. Insert an almond into each date.

Slowly melt the chocolate with the margarine over a bain-marie. Dip each date individually in the melted chocolate and transfer to a plate or a sheet of baking parchment. You can also dredge the chocolate-coated dates in grated chocolate if you want, and leave them to cool.

Chocolate and Hazelnut Pralines

Makes about 10
Difficulty ✱
Preparation time: 15 minutes plus
    cooling time

100 g/3¾ oz vegan dark chocolate
    (45–55 % cocoa solids)
75 g/6 tbsp vegan margarine
50 g/½ cup sifted icing sugar
100 g/scant 1 cup ground roasted
    hazelnuts (see tip)

Slowly melt the chocolate with the margarine over a bain-marie or in the microwave. Add the icing sugar and ground hazelnuts, stir briskly while over the bain-marie.

Allow the mixture to cool completely before shaping into pralines. Keep refrigerated until use.

Tip

If you can't find roasted ground hazelnuts, you can use the unroasted variety and roast them yourself in a dry non-stick frying pan for a few minutes.

Oat and Chocolate Crunchies with Sunflower Seeds

These crunchies make a great snack for when you're on the go or between meals, and they're really quick to make.

Makes about 30 small crunchies
Difficulty ✱
Preparation time: 10 minutes

25 g/2 tbsp refined coconut oil
3 tbsp sunflower seeds
6 tbsp coarse oatmeal (see note on p. 72)
35 g/1¼ oz vegan dark chocolate (45–55 %
    cocoa solids)
1 tbsp concentrated pear juice or maple
    syrup

Heat the coconut oil in a non-stick frying pan. Add the sunflower seeds and oatmeal, turn the heat to medium, and toast until light golden.

Remove from the heat, add the chocolate and concentrated pear juice and stir until the chocolate is fully melted and is evenly distributed. Leave to stand for 1 more minute. Spread the mixture out over a sheet of baking parchment and make sure there are no large clumps. Leave to cool for at least 10 minutes.
(Picture on p. 102)

Chocolate and Hazelnut Pralines

Oat and Chocolate Crunchies with Sunflower Seeds

Chocolate Sushi

Chocolate Sushi

A sweet reinterpretation of the classic Japanese dish.

Makes 4 rolls of each variety

Difficulty ✳✳✳

Preparation time: 45 minutes plus at least 2 hours
  cooling time

For the chocoholic makizushi:

About 215 g/1¾ cups ripe kiwifruit, strawberries,
  mango, pears, grapes or any combination of
  these fruits

100 g/3¾ oz vegan dark chocolate (45–55 %
  cocoa solids)

150 g/¾ cup sushi rice or rice pudding

1 tsp lemon juice

2 tbsp sugar

For the chocoholic California rolls:

White sesame seeds

About 215 g/1¾ cups ripe kiwifruit, strawberries,
  mango, pears, grapes or any combination of
  these fruits

100 g/3¾ oz vegan dark chocolate (45–55 %
  cocoa solids)

150 g/¾ cup sushi rice or rice pudding

1 tsp lemon juice

2 tbsp sugar

For the chocoholic makizushi, prepare a clean and smooth work surface.

Draw four rectangles measuring 17 x 11 cm/6½ x 4¼ in and four more of 17 x 10 cm/6½ x 4 in with a pencil on baking parchment and cut them out.

Wash or peel and clean the fruit, as required, and slice thinly. Slowly melt the chocolate over a bain-marie (not in the microwave because the chocolate will be too thick for this recipe).

In the meantime, bring 175 ml/¾ cup of water and the sushi rice to the boil in a small saucepan. Lower the temperature, cover with a lid and simmer for 10 minutes. Remove from the heat, remove the lid, and leave the rice to stand for 15 minutes. Add the lemon juice and sugar and mix well.

Now, use a quarter of the melted chocolate to coat the four 17 x 10 cm/6½ x 4 in rectangles completely, including the edges. Spread the still warm sushi rice over one of the 17 x 11 cm/6½ x 4¼ in rectangles, leaving a 1 cm/½ in border at the top and bottom along the longer edges without covering. Make a thin line of fruit of your choice (don't use too much fruit) along the middle of the rice, parallel to the longer edge. Roll the rice with the parchment, starting from one of the longer sides. It should come loose from the paper. Lay the rice roll over the chocolate-covered baking parchment with the edges flush, and then roll the chocolate over the top of the rice. Roll this parchment up slowly and carefully to the edge, and leave it on. Ideally, the ends of the paper should be quite flush.

With the help of a large knife, lay the rolls (baking parchment still attached), as they are made, on a plate with the join underneath, and refrigerate for 2 hours.

After cooling, carefully remove the baking parchment from the rolls. Use a sharp knife to cut the rolls into slices of about 2 cm/¾ in wide, dipping the knife in hot water between cuts. The chocoholic makizushi is ready.

For the chocoholic California roll, prepare a clean and smooth work surface.

Draw four 17 x 13 cm/6½ x 5 in rectangles on a sheet of baking parchment and cut them out. Sprinkle the work surface with sesame seeds. The sushi rolls will be rolled in it later.

Wash or peel and clean the fruit, as required, and slice thinly. Slowly melt the chocolate over a bain-marie (see opposite).

Prepare the sushi rice as described opposite.

Spread the still warm sushi rice over one of the four 17 x 11 cm/6½ x 4¼ in rectangles, leaving a 1 cm/½ in border at the top and bottom along the longer edges without covering. Spread the runny chocolate over the rice, also leaving a 1 cm/½ in border without covering, otherwise the chocolate will run out. Make a thin line of fruit of your choice (don't use too much fruit) along the middle of the rice, parallel to the longer edge.

Roll the rice with the parchment, starting from one of the longer sides. It should come loose from the paper. As they are made, carefully lay the rolls over the sprinkled sesame seeds, and use both hands to carefully turn them in the sesame seeds. With the help of a large flat knife, transfer the rolls to a plate. Refrigerate the sushi rolls for at least 2 hours.

After cooling, use a sharp knife to cut the rolls into slices of about 2 cm/¾ in wide, dipping the knife in hot water between cuts. (Picture on p. 103)

Tips

Precision is crucial for the success of this recipe. It is important that the rice is still hot and the chocolate is still runny when starting to make the rolls. It's a good idea to keep the saucepan/bain-marie with the chocolate close at hand and the chocolate over the bain-marie so it stays runny as you work.

To prevent the chocolate and/or the rice from cooling too soon, always make one roll at a time. Don't spread all the rice or chocolate over the baking parchment rectangles at the beginning.

A tip about cutting: The rolls are easier to cut if you take them out of the refrigerator about half an hour beforehand, as the chocolate will be less brittle. Also, don't cut the rolls slowly. Instead cut quickly by pressing the knife down from top to bottom.

Frozen Caramel and Truffle Tart 🌾 🥜

Warning, addictive! This recipe requires you to have sufficient space in your freezer.

For a tart with a diameter of about
    26 cm/10¼ in
Difficulty ✳✳
Preparation time: 25 minutes plus at least 3
    hours freezing time

For the cream:
150 g/5 oz vegan dark chocolate (45–55 %
    cocoa solids)
60 g/5 tbsp cashew butter or white
    almond butter
⅓ tsp salt

For the caramel:
300 ml/1¼ cups coconut milk
225 g/1 cup sugar
1 tsp lemon juice

For the cream, slowly melt the chocolate over a bain-marie. Add the cashew butter and mix well, keeping the bowl over the bain-marie. Add 50 ml/¼ cup of water and the salt, and slowly but thoroughly mix until smooth. Take the bowl off the bain-marie and transfer the cream to a shallow mould lined with baking parchment. Leave to cool for a short time, and then put the mould in the freezer for at least 1 hour.

For the caramel, combine 200 ml/scant 1 cup of coconut milk with the sugar and lemon juice in a saucepan and bring to the boil over a high heat. Slightly reduce the heat while keeping at a vigorous boil, and stir constantly with a whisk until the colour changes from white to light brown (this should take about 5 minutes). Be very careful because this change is very sudden. When hardly any more bubbles come up, this is a sign that it is almost ready.

Then continue to cook until the caramel turns a deep golden colour. If you remove the caramel from the heat too soon, it will be too light and its flavour won't be very intense, but you don't want it to cook for too long and become too dark. Now add the rest of the coconut milk, return the saucepan to the heat and stir the cream constantly for 2 minutes until smooth.

Immediately spread the liquid caramel (this is important) over the chocolate cream layer and immediately return the mould to the freezer for at least 2 hours.

Tip

Making caramel takes a little practice, so don't despair if it isn't perfect the first time.

Chocolate and Corn Flake Crunchies with Orange and Sea Salt

These crunchies are extremely fast to make. Don't store them in a plastic container or with cling film, otherwise they will lose all their crunch.
It's better to use a metal container, or leave them uncovered.

Makes 12
Difficulty *
Preparation time: 15 minutes

115 g/4 oz vegan dark chocolate
    (45–55 % cocoa solids)
20 g/1½ tbsp vegan margarine
2 tbsp orange juice
35 g/scant ½ cup corn flakes
40 g/½ cup candied orange peel
about ½ tsp coarse sea salt

Slowly melt the chocolate with the margarine over a bain-marie. Add the orange juice and mix to a smooth cream, keeping the bowl over the bain-marie.

Mix the cornflakes, candied orange peel and sea salt in a bowl. Pour the melted chocolate over the mixture and slowly mix. Use a tablespoon to form 12 compact mounds, space them out over a sheet of baking parchment and leave to cool completely.

Raspberry and Cocoa Ice Shake

Totally refreshing and with a light cocoa taste. Using frozen fruit is essential to ensure the shake is at the ideal temperature.
Best served ice cold with a straw.

Makes 330 ml (1 glass)
Difficulty *
Preparation time: 5 minutes

90 g/¾ cup frozen raspberries
25 g/2 tbsp white almond butter
150 ml/⅔ cup water
2 ice cubes
¼ tsp Bourbon vanilla powder
¾ tsp lightly defatted cocoa powder
2–3 tsp concentrated pear juice or
    maple syrup

Combine all the ingredients in a deep and narrow container, blend with a hand-held blender, and serve immediately.

Chocolate and Corn Flake Crunchies
with Orange and Sea Salt

Coconut Hot Chocolate

Cold Blueberry Breakfast Shake

Coconut Hot Chocolate

It doesn't have to be winter for this chocolate drink to lift your spirits.
The combination of coconut and chocolate is definitely one of my favourites.

Makes 250 ml/1 cup (serves 1)
Difficulty ✳
Preparation time: 5 minutes

200 ml/scant 1 cup coconut milk
25 ml/1½ tbsp agave syrup or 2 tbsp
    sugar
1–2 tsp lemon juice
4 tsp desiccated coconut
25 g/1 oz vegan dark chocolate
    (45–55 % cocoa), grated

Combine all the ingredients in a small saucepan, place over the heat, and stir slowly and constantly until the chocolate is completely melted. Serve immediately.
(Picture on p. 110)

Cold Blueberry Breakfast Shake

Fancy a bit of variety at breakfast? Here you have it.
This shake is definitely what you're after.
Combine it with oat and chocolate crunchies for a light and enjoyable start to your day, especially in summer.
This shake also makes a fantastic dessert.
Variety guaranteed.

Makes 330 ml/ 1⅓ cups (serves 1)
Difficulty ✳
Preparation time: 20 minutes

100–125 g/scant 1 cup – generous
    cup blueberries
25 g/2 tbsp white almond butter
2 tbsp concentrated pear juice or
    maple syrup
1 tsp vanilla sugar or ⅓ tsp Bourbon vanilla
    powder
1 tbsp lemon juice
120 ml/½ cup water, as cold as
    possible

Oat and chocolate crunchies with
    sunflower seeds (see recipe on
    p.100)

Wash, clean and dry the berries. Combine all the ingredients, except the oat and chocolate crunchies, in a deep and narrow container, and blend with a hand-held blender. Serve with the oat and chocolate crunchies.
(Picture on p. 111)

Chocolate and Pineapple Cream

Serves 3–4
Difficulty *
Preparation time: 5 minutes plus at
    least 4 hours cooling time

250 ml/1 cup soya milk
1½ tbsp lightly defatted cocoa
    powder
125 g/generous 1 cup tinned
    pineapple
4 tbsp pineapple juice (from the
    tin)
60 g/5 tbsp refined coconut oil,
    melted
45 g/scant ¼ cup sugar
1 pinch salt
3 (10 g/0.35 oz) sachets whipped
    cream stabiliser

Combine all the ingredients in a large, deep mixing jug
and blend well for 3–4 minutes. Refrigerate for at least
4 hours.
(Picture on p. 114)

Avocado and Chocolate Buttercream with Orange and Black Pepper

This is probably the healthiest chocolate cream
you can imagine.
In addition to iron and calcium, avocados are high
in vitamins A and B, unsaturated fats and other
nutrients, and leave you feeling sated longer.

Serves 2–3
Difficulty *
Preparation time: 5 minutes

80 g/3¼ oz vegan dark chocolate
    (45–55 % cocoa solids)
1 ripe avocado
1 untreated orange, for juice and grated zest
⅓ tsp sea salt
2 tbsp maple syrup or 2½ tbsp icing sugar
Freshly ground pepper

Slowly and completely melt the chocolate in the
microwave or over a bain-marie.
    Halve the avocado, remove the stone and scoop out
the flesh.
    Combine the avocado with the other ingredients in a
deep and narrow container. Add the melted chocolate
and blend well with a hand-held blender.
    The cream can be served immediately or kept in the
refrigerator until later.
(Picture on p. 115)

Chocolate and Pineapple Cream

Avocado and Chocolate Buttercream
with Orange and Black Pepper

Home-Made Chocolate Yoghurt

My favourite yoghurt has always been the chocolate-flavoured variety. But unfortunately, there are no satisfactory vegan alternatives available to buy.

This recipe allows you to make your own chocolate yoghurt, and it leaves all other shop-bought versions in the shade.

You can also use sweetened yoghurt as the base for this recipe, as some supermarkets only offer this. In this case, simply leave out the additional sugar in the recipe.

Makes 600 g
Difficulty ✳
Preparation time: 10 minutes plus at least 1 hour cooling time

For the quick and easy version:
80 g/3¼ oz vegan dark chocolate (45–55 % cocoa solids)
100 ml/scant ½ cup soya milk
400 g/2 cups natural soya yoghurt, unsweetened
1 tsp sugar
⅔ tsp vanilla sugar

For the deluxe version:
125 g/4 oz vegan dark chocolate (45–55 % cocoa solids)
120 ml/½ cup soya milk
400 g/2 cups natural soya yoghurt, unsweetened
1 tsp sugar
⅔ tsp vanilla sugar
1 tsp lightly defatted cocoa powder

For the quick and easy version, combine the chocolate and soya milk in a saucepan and heat while stirring constantly, until the chocolate is completely melted. Combine with the other ingredients in a bowl and mix well (preferably with a whisk) and leave to cool completely.

Store in the refrigerator. This yoghurt can keep in the refrigerator for 1–2 weeks.

For the deluxe version, combine the chocolate and soya milk in a saucepan and heat while stirring constantly, until the chocolate is completely melted. Put 3 tablespoons of the chocolate mixture in a bowl and add the yoghurt, sugar and vanilla sugar. Mix briskly and thoroughly (preferably with a whisk) until smooth.

Combine 2 tablespoons of the yoghurt mixture and cocoa powder with the remaining 3 tablespoons of melted chocolate in a saucepan and mix to obtain a dark cream.

Pour the dark cream into the bottom of two or three glasses, then use a spoon to cover it with the lighter yoghurt cream. Refrigerate for at least 1 hour.

Chocolate Risotto with Raspberry Sauce

Serves 2

Difficulty ✳

Preparation time: 1 hour

For the risotto:

750 ml/3 cups almond or soya milk

The seeds from ½ vanilla pod

1½ tbsp sugar

1 pinch salt

125 g/⅝ cup risotto rice

40–50 g/1½–2 oz vegan dark chocolate (45–55 % cocoa solids, depending on how strong you like it)

1 tbsp cognac (optional)

Cocoa powder and a few raspberries (optional) to decorate

For the raspberry sauce:

225 g/generous 1¾ cups raspberries (see tip)

1½–2 tbsp sugar

1 tbsp lemon juice

For the risotto, combine the almond or soya milk with the vanilla seeds, sugar and salt, and bring to the boil. Sprinkle in the rice, cover and cook, stirring from time to time, until the rice has absorbed almost all the liquid (about 40 minutes). About 10 minutes before the end of the cooking time, add the chocolate and if you like stir in the cognac.

For the raspberry sauce, wash, clean and dry the raspberries, and purée with a hand-held blender. Heat the sugar in a frying pan and make a golden caramel. Add the puréed raspberries and reduce for 2–3 minutes until the caramelised sugar has completely dissolved from the bottom of the pan. Stir in the lemon juice.

Serve the risotto in a small bowl and decorate with a few fresh raspberries if you like. Pour the sauce over the rice and dust with cocoa powder.

Tip

If you don't like the idea of having raspberry seeds in the sauce, simply press the puréed raspberries through a sieve.

Chocolate and Chilli Meatballs with a Quick Tomato Salsa

Serves 2

Difficulty ∗

Preparation time: 20 minutes

For the meatballs:

250 g/9 oz tofu

50 g/1 cup dry breadcrumbs

2 tbsp wheat or spelt flour

1 tsp soy sauce

1 level tsp salt

2 tsp lemon juice

½ tbsp smooth mustard

1 tsp sweet paprika

25 g/1 oz vegan dark chocolate (45–55 % cocoa solids), finely grated

½–1 small chilli pepper, finely chopped

Peanut (groundnut) oil or high oleic sunflower oil

For the salsa:

2 large ripe tomatoes, finely diced

1 small onion, finely chopped

1½ tbsp chopped fresh basil

2 tsp freshly squeezed lemon juice

About ¾ tsp salt

Freshly ground pepper

Mix all the ingredients for the salsa in a bowl and leave to stand for 10 minutes.

For the meatballs, combine all the ingredients, except the oil, in a large bowl. Knead vigorously with both hands for 3–5 minutes. Thorough kneading is crucial for the success of this dish. Shape the mixture into small balls.

Heat a generous amount of oil in a non-stick frying pan and fry the meatballs over a medium–high heat for about 5 minutes. There should always be sufficient oil in the pan. Top up the oil if necessary. Serve the meatballs with the salsa.

Tip

For a decorative effect, garnish the meatballs with chilli threads.

Chestnut and Tofu Schnitzel with a Red Wine and Chocolate Sauce

Serves 2, makes 5–6 small patties
Difficulty ∗
Preparation time: 35 minutes

For the schnitzel:
200 g/1¾ cups frozen, peeled chestnuts or
    vacuum-packed cooked chestnuts
200 g/7 oz firm tofu
1 tbsp lemon juice
1½ tsp untreated lemon zest
Freshly ground pepper
1 level tsp salt
2 tsp cornflour
3 tbsp light wheat or spelt flour
2 tsp quality balsamic vinegar
1 tbsp chopped fresh parsley
Refined olive oil for frying
Salt

For the red wine and chocolate sauce:
1 small onion, finely chopped
1 tbsp olive oil
½ tsp cornflour
50 ml/¼ cup cold water
1 tsp vegetable stock powder
150 ml/⅔ cup red wine
1 tsp quality balsamic vinegar
10 g/2 tsp white almond butter
2 squares vegan dark chocolate (45–55 %
    cocoa solids)
1–2 tsp fresh thyme leaves (optional)
Salt, freshly ground pepper

For the schnitzel, if you're using frozen chestnuts, put them in a saucepan and cover with water. Cover with the lid, place over medium heat and cook for about 15 minutes, until they are soft and falling apart. If you're using vacuum-packed chestnuts, they can be used as they are for the next step, where they are kneaded with the other ingredients.

Drain the cooked chestnuts well and combine with the rest of the ingredients, except the olive oil, in a bowl. Leave to cool if necessary. Vigorously knead the ingredients together for at least 3 minutes. Shape the mixture into 5–6 large patties.

Heat the olive oil in a frying pan and fry the schnitzel over medium–high heat for 4 minutes on each side until golden brown and crispy. Don't touch the schnitzels when frying for the first 2 minutes. Even after turning, leave them alone for the first 1–2 minutes. Note: There must always be enough oil in the pan, otherwise the schnitzels will stick to the bottom. Top up the oil if necessary.

For the sauce, sweat the chopped onions in the oil until translucent. Dissolve the cornflour completely in cold water. Add the cornflour and other ingredients to the onions in the pan, and simmer uncovered over a medium heat. Season with salt and freshly ground pepper.

Seitan Ragout with Chocolate and Dried Apricots

Serves 2
Difficulty *
Preparation time: 45 minutes

2–3 tbsp peanut (groundnut) oil or high oleic
    sunflower oil
200 g/7 oz seitan, cut into strips
1 large onion, cut into fine strips
1 large carrot, cut into fine strips
4 juniper berries
175 ml/¾ cup good red wine
1 tsp vegetable stock powder
4 squares vegan dark chocolate (45–55 %
    cocoa solids)
2 tsp tomato purée
250 ml/1 cup water
1 dried bay leaf
2 unsulphured dried apricots, cut into strips (see
    tip)
8–10 sprigs fresh rosemary
1–2 dash(es) lemon juice
5 g/1 tsp white almond butter (optional)
About ¾ tsp salt
Freshly ground pepper

Heat the oil over a high heat in a non-stick frying pan and sear the seitan for 4 minutes. Add the onion strips and fry for 2 minutes. Top up the oil if necessary.

Add the rest of the ingredients, reduce the heat to low–medium and half cover the pan. Cook for 20–30 minutes, stirring occasionally, until the carrots are soft. Season with salt and freshly ground pepper.

This dish can be served with *rösti*, sautéed potatoes or pasta.

Tip

Unsulphured dried apricots can be distinguished by their characteristic brown colour. More aromatic than the bright orange, sulphured apricots, they don't just make a healthy snack, but also work well in savoury dishes.

Recipe index